Praise for *The Influencing Formula*

"The Larson duo has succeeded once again in authoring this essential text for business analysts and project managers. The Influencing Formula provides tried-and-true tools and techniques, and some that are even magical. Anyone who has a leadership role in contemporary projects designed to drive business innovation should have the Larsons' indispensable book on their shelves."

Kitty Hass, PMP
Author of *The Enterprise Business Analyst*

"I have been a long-time advocate of meaningfully involving sponsors and clients in their project. It is difficult, but essential to project success, especially implementation. Here is a book that will create awareness about how to establish effective client relationships between the PM or BA and their sponsoring agency.

The Larsons have given us solid advice on how to interact with the sponsor and the client that I personally recommend. I will be able to add practices that will strengthen my client relationship efforts. Whatever your client relations situation, you will benefit too.

I especially liked Chapter 7 on consultative questioning. The authors set the stage for what might be called an "empathetic dialogue". Their structure bears remarkable similarity to the principles of Solution Selling and I know from personal experience that it does works well. For me, that is worth the price of the book!"

Robert K. Wysocki, PhD, President EII Publi
Author of *Effective Project Management: Traditi*

D1224063

"Lack of authority is the single biggest complaint I hear from project managers and business analysts. This book addresses the problem head on. The job requires influence, not authority. The person with the most influence has the most power. You don't need to be the boss to have influence. I could open this book to any part, start reading, and get value. Any page could be a seminar session and every idea is thought-provoking and effective. For project teams, influence is power. The goal is to get the job done. Working with people in an influential way is essential and this book helps you get there.

People think that you need to be in authority to be held accountable. The reality is we are accountable for all sorts of things we cannot control. When I look back on my career, I was probably most effective and most creative when I lacked authority and had to work hard to become influential. Conversely, when I had real authority I was less effective because I did not have to work so hard to influence people. When you lack authority you have to collaborate with others and work hard to achieve something."

Steven Wille, MBA, PMP
Author of *Colorful Leadership*

"There is really no "formula" for influence and authority; if it were that simple, it would have been bottled and sold years ago. However, the Larsons have accomplished the Biology class equivalent of these difficult concepts and dissected them in a way that the most novice project leader (be it a PM or a BA) can break down the components and begin using them immediately. Moreover, the most experienced PM or BA can pick it up and be reminded of the critical soft skills necessary for success. Filled with stories and experience of the rich-shared history of Richard and Elizabeth, this book is destined to become a "must have" on every project library."

Timothy L. Johnson, PMP
Author of *Race Through the Forest: A Project Management Fable*

the Influencing FORMULA

How to Become a Trusted Advisor
and Influence Without Authority

Elizabeth Larson and Richard Larson

*This book is dedicated to **Harvey Mild,** who taught us both about the importance of influencing without authority*

Acknowledgements

We want to thank Andrea Brockmeier, Susan Heidorn, Stevie Peterson, Bob Prentiss, and JoAnne Sabin for their contributions to Watermark Learning's Influencing Skills curriculum. We also want to thank the entire Watermark Learning staff for their patience and support.

OUR STORY

Today, employers are looking for more than` just job expertise. They need problem solvers—highly-performing professionals with the practical know-how to create enduring results.

Since 1992, Watermark Learning has been cultivating today's problem solvers and tomorrow's leaders through Project Management, Business Analysis, Influencing Skills, and Business Process Management training. Our clients receive skill development that enables both organizations and individuals to define, analyze, and recommend solutions that produce bottom-line results.

Experience our unique combination of best practices, practical approach, and engaging delivery and you'll discover why organizations prefer the Watermark Learning portfolio of training services.

TRAINING SERVICES

Live Training: Our instructor-led courses cover today's most relevant topics to help you keep pace in today's demanding business environment. Classes are offered in a traditional classroom setting or through virtual delivery using the internet.

Private Classes: Minimize scheduling hassles and travel expenses by inviting a Watermark Learning expert to your site. Your project team will benefit from lower per-student cost and personalized curriculum that incorporates your organization's particular method and corporate culture.

Public Classes: When you need to train one person or a few people, our open-enrollment classes provide you flexibility. We offer several iterations of core classes throughout the year. You can "sample" our training before committing to an onsite class.

Courseware Licensing: Jump-start your own training programs by licensing our high-quality course materials. Teach classes with your own instructors, customize them to your needs, or contract with us for a turnkey solution.

Mentoring/Consultative Training: Reinforce your classroom learning and enhance job performance through our mentoring services. We help you tackle your unique needs while helping you keep projects on track.

Certification Programs: If you want a skill-based Business Analysis or Project Management program, obtain a Masters Certificate from Auburn University and expand your career horizons. If you desire an industry certification from PMI® or IIBA®, we offer best-in-class PMP® and CBAP®/CCBA® programs.

"Course materials were clear and concise and exercises were excellent—makes sense in my real world. The instructor was also very, very good—shared knowledge and experiences with us without making that the central point. Every minute was valuable. Thanks!"

MICHELLE WEBB
ALLIANZ LIFE INSURANCE

Watermark Learning
7301 Ohms Lane
Minneapolis, MN 55439
Tel +1 952-921-0900 · 800-646-9362
www.WatermarkLearning.com

Contents

List of Figures

List of Tables

THE INFLUENCING FORMULA

This unique project-focused book on influencing is packed with countless practical tips, techniques, and examples of how to influence without authority. The authors together have amassed over 60 years of first-hand experience running projects and doing business analysis in small, medium, and large organizations. Their experience as practitioners, combined with over 20 years of running their company, Watermark Learning, provides them with a realistic and proven base of knowledge and skills for being influential. They packaged their combined experience into a concept they call *"The Influencing Formula"* and share it with other project professionals.

> BONUS: The book covers over a dozen tools and techniques, which are available as free, downloadable templates to those who purchase the book. See Appendix B for instructions.

Features

- Use a ten-question self-assessment questionnaire to determine if you are ready to be a trusted advisor.
- Learn how to harness the two main forms of power that project professionals can use to help influence the right decisions.
- Learn how to overcome the six common barriers to influencing without authority.

TRUST

- Learn numerous techniques to build trust with stakeholders, and avoid the most common ways to "bust" trust with them.
- Discover the top ten techniques for building trust and collaboration when you are physically separated in virtual teams.

PREPARATION

- Receive extensive coverage of six effective preparation techniques that will increase influence.
- Use a practical consulting method to help perform consultation and contribute to influencing stakeholders to do "the right thing."
- Uncover 12 proven tools to help with consultative preparation and greater influence, including over 100 consultative questions to choose from to help understand business needs and requirements for projects.

COURAGE

- Learn seven keys to being courageous and how to employ them effectively on projects.
- Discover five tips for gaining support for your ideas and recommendations.
- Find out the ten most common mistakes that project professionals make with difficult stakeholders and how to avoid them.
- Understand nine common project-related issues with difficult stakeholders and how to overcome them.

01 Introduction to Influencing

"Even if you don't have the authorities – and frankly I didn't have the authorities for anything – if you take charge, people will follow. Someone has to pull it all together."

HENRY PAULSON
FORMER US TREASURY SECRETARY

We often get asked, "How can we get stakeholders to attend our meetings?" or "How can we get stakeholders' buy-in on the project?" These are complex questions, and the simple answer is that *we can't.* As business analysts (BAs) and project managers (PMs) we can't **get** anyone to do anything, but we can certainly influence them so that they **want** to. Similarly, we hear other BAs complaining that they are given a solution and don't believe that they can step back and take the time to understand the business need. We're told, "I can't speak up when my sponsor sets the direction of the project" or "In our organization, they shoot the messenger." *How can we effectively influence when we have no authority to do so?*

We believe that there is an influencing formula that includes building trust, being prepared, and having an overabundance of courage, and if we have those three ingredients, we will be able to exert a great deal of influence in our organizations.

In future chapters, we explore each of these concepts in detail. To quickly introduce the three main components of our formula, see *Figure 1.* It shows the dimensions of trust, preparation, and courage.

FIGURE 1: The Influencing Formula

Terms, Terms, and More Terms

So what is influence and how does it differ from, let's say, persuasion or manipulation? What is authority?

Let's start with the term "influence," which comes from the Latin root "influens," which means "to flow in." When we influence, then, we want our ideas to flow into others; that is, to become a part of them. That's different from "persuade," which comes from the Latin root "persuadere," which means "to urge."

Influence is more of a *transference* and persuasion more *presenting* an argument to convince others to change their thoughts, their feelings, or their actions. Personally, we as authors prefer influencing to urging because it feels more consultative to us.

Another distinction we are often asked to make is the relationship between influencing and manipulating, the latter meaning, among other things, to "influence skillfully, especially in an unfair manner." The word manipulate comes from the Latin "manipulus," meaning "handful." We have to say that, in our experience, people who try to manipulate us are certainly a handful!

As project professionals, we do not manipulate others. But how do we know that we're influencing and not manipulating?

We need to ask ourselves two questions: first, why am I trying to influence someone; and second, is it for the good of the organization?

If we want to influence someone because it will help the project meet its objectives and help the organization achieve its goals, rather than for personal gain, then chances are we are influencing, not manipulating. This concept aligns with the definition from *A Guide to the Project Management Body of Knowledge 4th ed.* (PMBOK): "Influencing is a strategy of sharing power and relying on interpersonal skills to get others to cooperate towards common goals."[1]

Do BAs and PMs Have Power?

Authority is the "power or right to control, judge, or prohibit the actions of others."[2]

So far so good, but what is power?

It's "the ability to do or act."[3] Ah, so here we have the crux of the matter. As project professionals, we do have power with the ability to act, but we do not have authority, which is another type of power.

A narrower definition comes from the *PMBOK® Guide*, Chapter 10.1.2.1: power is the ability to impose one's will.

Can PMs and BAs impose their will? We think that indeed they not only can, but that they do. There are different ways we impose our will. There are six common forms of power. Some are weak, having short-term effects. Others have long-lasting effects and are therefore strong.

Table 1 lists the six forms of power from weakest to strongest and provides an explanation and example of each.[4]

Type of Power	Definition	Example
Coercive	Punishment—the proverbial stick.	"If you don't work overtime, you will not be able to take a vacation."
Referent	Reliance on another source (e.g., name-dropping).	"I'm not happy about this deadline either, but the sponsor says it needs to be done by this date."
Reward	Inducement—the proverbial carrot.	"If you work overtime, we'll give you a bonus."
Positional/ legitimate/ authority	This type of power comes from one's position in the organization. This is what we mean by "authority."	"For better or worse, I'm the sponsor and a VP, and this is the budget I've approved."
Expert	Use of skills and knowledge.	"We need more time to install these PCs. My records show that this is how long it takes."
Personal or Leadership	This is the inner power that allows leaders to stand up for what they believe, along with the interpersonal skills and charisma needed to inspire and motivate others.	"I'll go with you to talk to the sponsor. I bet we can get her to approve more resources."

TABLE 1: Forms of Power

What this means is that, as project professionals, we BAs and PMs have certain types of power and not others, although the exact ones might vary by organization. Most of us do not have reward, coercive, or positional power (authority). We can rely on referent power, but unless it is combined with personal power, it is weak and short-lived.

TIP

Generally speaking, we need to rely on two types of power to get others to act—expert and personal.

Therefore, generally speaking, we need to rely on two types of power to get others to act—expert and personal. Fortunately, these are the strongest and longest-lasting forms of power.

What do we say to the project professional whose inclination is to be an order-taker, such as the BA who is reluctant to push back against the sponsor about the business need? We would not argue with our sponsors or any key stakeholder. We would try to influence them—*a big difference.*

We recall the adage we heard years ago: "Our sponsors aren't always right, but they are always our sponsors." How can we effectively influence them? Here are some simple rules:

1. **Figure out how to build trust** and strengthen the relationship with our sponsors and key stakeholders, because trying to influence without trust might not be possible. Remember that building the relationship is more than "schmoozing." Sponsors might have neither the time nor the inclination to accept an offer to meet and greet or have lunch with us, and there are more effective ways to build trust (See Chapter 3, Building Trust).

2. **Know what you're talking about.** We need to rely on our business and professional expertise and past successes, as well as risks and horror stories from past projects. If we try to tap dance without being prepared, we risk our credibility, and when that's gone, influencing will not be possible. See Chapters 4-8 for ideas and techniques to develop influential preparation skills.

3. **Have** the **courage to recommend the right thing.** We as authors have never been criticized for recommending what we thought was best for the organization or project. That's not to say we have remained unscathed from trying unsuccessfully to do battle. But if we're honest with ourselves, our scars have come not from trying to influence but from the battles. Arguing and becoming emotionally attached to a position or result tends to leave scars. Likewise, we've been burned trying to change people's minds through persuasion. We've rarely been criticized, though, for recommending the right thing.

That's our "formula" then—trust plus preparation times courage. In this book, we will discuss the complexities related to building trust, preparing to influence, and having the courage to do the right thing.

---

1   Project Management Institute, *A Guide to the Project Management Body of Knowledge (PMBOK® Guide)*, 4th ed. Appendix G5, (Newtown Square, PA: Project Management Inst, 2008), 151.

2   Dictionary.com, accessed July 30, 2012, http://dictionary.reference.com/browse/authority?s=t.

3   Dictionary.com, accessed July 30, 2012, http://dictionary.reference.com/browse/power?s=t.

4   Adapted from: J. French & B.H. Raven. Studies of Social Power, Institute for Social Research, Ann Arbor, MI (1959). accessed August 20, 2012, http://books.google.com/books?hl=en&lr=&id=DL2AsvuzJHUC&oi=fnd&pg=PA61&dq=studies+of+social+power&ots=hOxA4ure7E&sig=-nNZ79YYnhxHsBoBwS6ouDQwpd8#v=onepage&q=studies%20of%20social%20power&f=false.

02 Influence and Authority

"The key to successful leadership today is influence, not authority."

KEN BLANCHARD

MANAGEMENT AUTHORITY

In the earlier chapter, we saw the distinction between influence and authority and looked at the different types of power we have available to us and the types we may not have. We also discussed the importance of using the types of power that we have.

In this chapter, we will discuss barriers to effective influencing, various types of influence, different ways we influence others, some influencing models and how they can be used effectively, the use of social media to influence, and creating an environment where people feel empowered to positively influence the organization.

Finally, we will introduce the concept of the trusted advisor and how business analysts and project managers can fulfill that role.

Background

There are a myriad of useful books and articles on the subject of how to effectively influence others. Gary Yuki and J.B. Tracy wrote an article on influencing tactics.[1] We will present practical applications of these concepts later in this chapter. Allan Cohen and David Bradford have written extensively on the subject of influencing without authority. Their influence model based on reciprocity and exchange discusses how to "get what you want, especially from people over whom you have no authority."[2] We will briefly discuss this concept also in this chapter.

Chris Argyris' Ladder of Inference describes the difference between perception and reality. Although we humans start with observable data, our perceptions are based on our assumptions and the data we selectively choose.

We cannot change how we are perceived, but we can change how we perceive others.[3]

Maister, Green, and Galford's *The Trusted Advisor* provides a practical approach to individuals acting as external consultants. Their tips are presented in handy lists and written from both the consultant's and client's perspectives.[4]

Barriers to Influencing

We all know that we should do the right thing for our projects, our business units, and our organization. So what's stopping us?

There are myriad obstacles, both organizational and personal, that prevent us from being effective influencers. Here are some common ones.

1. Organizational Structure

One obstacle is a hierarchical organizational and communications structure. Many of us work in organizations that are more command and control than collaborative. The organizational structure tends to be hierarchical. That is, there are clear lines of "authority." Communications tends to be more top-down, coming from the executives or "those in charge" to the workers. And even in organizations with open-door policies, where workers are free to bypass their managers to express concerns or recommend changes, the staff usually goes through a formal chain of command. In addition, many national cultures favor a more formal communications structure, presenting a barrier to effective influence.

2. Organizational Culture

Some organizational cultures are more competitive than collaborative. Business units, divisions, or agencies compete for scarce resources. In these situations, it is not uncommon for each sub-organization to have its own goals and agendas. Even when the goals of the sub-organizations are aligned with the overall organizational goals, the competition among these units and agencies is fierce. Therefore, the way they go about achieving their goals may conflict with another business unit or agency.

In other organizational cultures, expressing concerns, identifying risks, and making recommendations for changes is not encouraged. The staff in these organizations that do so are sometimes told they do not have a "can-do" attitude. They may be signaled out in meetings or publically humiliated. Such intimidating behavior almost ensures that the staff keeps silent, which not only stifles creativity but also promotes stagnation. Even when the organization as a whole is more creative and collaborative, there might be business units whose cultures discourage speaking out.

3. Time

Following the influencing formula takes time. Building relationships and trust cannot be accomplished quickly. It requires consistency over time. If we betray the trust, it will take time to restore it.

Knowing what we're talking about also takes time. In order to become an expert, to prepare for our influencing interactions, and to perform the necessary analysis to be credible and to be able to answer questions all takes more time than most of us have.

The challenge is, of course, that both building trust and being prepared take time away from our tasks at hand. With tight deadlines and more to get done than we can possibly do, with every email generating what seems like an infinite number of others, many of us are not inclined to take the time for effective influencing.

4. Winging It

While many of us see the benefits of planning, some prefer to be or are best at being in react mode. They are masters at reacting but resist planning. Often these influencers are marvelous tap-dancers who rely on the force of their personal magnetism rather than their expertise. For them, influencing tends to be informal. While this approach might be effective for some, it is less effective for most of us who need to prepare in order to have the confidence to respond appropriately.

5. Political Landscape

One of the barriers to effective influencing is being oblivious to the political landscape that constantly evolves in every organization. Likewise, if we are new to an organization, these political considerations take time to learn. Getting to know our stakeholders, their communications style, how to build trust and credibility with them, being able to navigate around the "water cooler coalitions," and being able to distinguish between the grapevine and the rumor mill all lead to more effective influencing.

6. Fear of Failure

One of the chief reasons that people do not influence is because they're afraid of being unsuccessful. They fear that a lack of success will be a negative reflection on them. These people don't have the confidence that they can influence. They let the barriers above stand in the way of trying to do what they know is right.

TIP

When we take the time to build trust and are thoroughly prepared, we will have the confidence to effectively influence.

We believe that when we take the time to build trust and when we are thoroughly prepared, we will have the confidence to effectively influence. We also need to redefine success. We may have failed to persuade in the past. But that doesn't mean that we have failed to influence. We might not have changed a decision. We might not have convinced a decision-maker to take a particular course of action. However, if we have followed the formula, we might have altered a decision-maker's thoughts and/or feelings. We will look further into this fear factor in Chapter 8, Developing the Courage to Be Influential.

Approaches to Influencing[5]

When we influence, we have an effect on others' thoughts, feelings, and/or actions. There are different approaches that we can take to influence these aspects. Yuki and Tracy call these influence "tactics."[6]

The most effective influencing involves influencing both thoughts and behaviors in order to cause desired actions. Less effective influencing affects either thoughts or feelings, but not both. Most people have their favorite approaches and often use several.

> *"A good head and a good heart are always a formidable combination."*
>
> **NELSON MANDELA**

Here we discuss several influencing tactics and the ways in which they affect thoughts, feelings, and actions.

1. Rational Persuasion

Rational persuasion is the use of facts and figures to cause a change in how people think and therefore how they will act. It has been said to be "characterized by the use of logical arguments with factual information to persuade others that a particular action will lead to a particular outcome."[7] Many of the people we want to influence need to have quantifiable data before they will make decisions, relying more on logic than emotions. We will discuss this dichotomy later in the book.

There are many examples of rational persuasion, although the most effective influencers use it in conjunction with other approaches that change the emotions. Lawyers use logical persuasion to influence juries. Management consultants use logical persuasion to influence decision-makers. Politicians use logical persuasion when they cite statistics. Marketers use logical persuasion when they use facts in their advertisements. In short, rational persuasion by itself appeals to the thought/action combination.

2. Inspirational Appeal

Inspirational appeal is the use of arguments that appeal to feelings related to doing the right thing and appeals to the emotions and actions. When we have a vision, communicate that vision, and try to get others on board with that vision, we are using inspirational appeal, which is most effective when influencers match the appeal to the values of those being influenced.

Leaders have used inspirational appeal throughout history. A few examples of inspirational appeal are Martin Luther King, Jr.'s "I Have a Dream" speech, John F. Kennedy's 1961 inaugural speech that included the famous line "Ask not what your country can do for you, ask what you can do for your country," and the Chinese saying, "Do the impossible, for it may truly be possible. "[8]

3. Personal Appeal

Personal appeal is the use of influence based on a personal relationship. For example, one might say, "Come on. You're my brother. Won't you lend me the money I need for a new car?" However, we also think personal appeal is influence based on the force of one's personality.

People with charisma use personal appeal, which is often used in conjunction with other influence approaches. We often think of politicians when it comes to using personal appeal. Many organizational and national leaders have personal appeal, and it is often used in conjunction with inspirational appeal. Other examples include the use of well-known actors in advertisements and sports personalities used in brand endorsements.

4. Consultation

Consultation is the use of influence based on expert and personal power. Because consultation acts on thoughts, feelings, and actions, it is a strong approach. For consultation to be effective, it must follow the Influencing Formula based on trust, preparation, and courage. It involves analyzing problems and recommending solutions.

As a general rule, consultants ask questions and use active listening to understand the problem and its root cause. Because consultation acts on thoughts and feelings while encouraging action, it is one of the most effective forms of influence when the consultant is truly a trusted advisor. Doctors, lawyers, and management consultants all use consultation as a way to influence their clients.

5. Ingratiation

Ingratiation involves getting on the good side of the person being influenced. Most often it acts on emotions. An example of ingratiation is the character of Uriah Heap in Charles Dickens' novel, *David Copperfield*. In the story, a lawyer's assistant is able to influence the lawyer to make decisions with disastrous results by ingratiating himself to the lawyer and his family in order to take over the firm and marry the lawyer's daughter.

6. Forming a Coalition

Forming a coalition involves working with other like-minded individuals with similar goals to influence an outcome. Forming a coalition can act on feelings and actions. A few well-known examples include labor unions, political action committees, and homeowner associations.

7. Relentless Pressure

Relentless pressure involves persuasion through persistence. It acts mostly on feelings and actions. Examples include economic sanctions, war, and (often) pester power, the tactic teenagers use to try to influence their parents.

8. Reciprocity and Exchange

Cohen and Bradford have added reciprocity and exchange to the list of influencing tactics. The concept is that we can influence others by returning favors and by exchanging what we have for what they need. Reciprocity and exchange can act on thoughts, feelings, and actions, depending on what is given and what is received.

Table 2 combines the concepts of influence tactics with types of power and the appeal to thoughts, feelings, or actions.

Influence Approach	Thoughts	Feelings	Actions	Expertise	Leadership
Rational Persuasion	X		X	X	
Inspirational Appeal		X	X		X
Personal Appeal		X	X		X
Consultation	X	X	X	X	X
Ingratiation		X			
Coalitions		X	X		X
Relentless Pressure		X	X		
Reciprocity & Exchange	X	X	X		X

TABLE 2: Influence and Power

To summarize, we all try to get others to do what we want by influencing what people think and feel and, therefore, what they do. Some of the approaches we take will change people's thoughts, others act on their feelings, and others will change both.

A Practical Approach to the Five Currency Types

People almost universally participate in reciprocity. For example, we usually return dinner invitations to those who have invited us to dinner. If we continue to invite people to dinner without being invited in return, we might choose not to invite them in the future. However, how we reciprocate may vary from culture to culture.

Here is an example from when Elizabeth lived in Cuiaba, Brazil.

"When I first moved in, neighbors often stopped by and brought an item of food on a plate, ranging from a lone mango to a fancy dessert. I would wash the plate and promptly return it, thinking that the neighbor might want to use it right away. Later I would cook and bring something to them and the plate or pan that I used would always be returned with some kind of treat. After many strange looks whenever I returned a clean but empty plate, I asked around and was told that it was rude to return an empty dish. It didn't matter what was returned, but the plate should not be empty. This exchange was the norm for their culture."

Closely related to reciprocity, the principal of exchange has always been vital to our survival. We buy goods and services for money. We get paid for the work we do. We sometimes barter goods for other goods or services. The examples are far too numerous to list.

Cohen and Bradford base their influence model on this principle. They discuss five currency types in their book.[9] These currencies are things we can use in exchange for cooperation. In other words, when we want something from someone in a business situation, we can offer them one or more of these five currency types. For project professionals, this principle is useful in thinking about how we can obtain cooperation from stakeholders who do not work directly for us. The five currency types are described below:

1. Inspiration

There are three important aspects to this currency type: vision, excellence, and moral/ethical correctness. On a project, this currency can be used to provide an opportunity to work on a highly visible, strategic project. Or we might get a sponsor to approve more testing resources if we can assure them of a quality end-result. When we explain to a reluctant business expert why taking the time to define requirements is the right thing for the organization, we are appealing to their sense of correctness. For example, when a sponsor asked Elizabeth to manage a project that would give the organization an advantage over its leading competitor, she was immediately on board, even though she knew it would be a large, difficult project involving lots of overtime. She accepted the challenging project, which appealed to her because it supported the vision and strategic direction of the organization. And it offered personal gain because it would be a high priority project increasing the likelihood of obtaining future resources.

2. Position

There are five important aspects to this currency type: recognition, visibility, reputation, importance, and contacts. Although projects that support the strategic direction of the organization are often the most visible, not all are. The position currency is used for project managers and stakeholders who thrive on difficult, visible projects, because there is the chance to shine, to cement their reputations to handle challenges, and to gain visibility with the executives. The project noted above was a highly visible project, and that increased its appeal. In the beginning of that project, it was difficult to get some of the business subject matter experts (SMEs) to find the time to define their requirements for the new system. Once the project was underway and there was considerable excitement about it, many of these reluctant stakeholders found a way to make time in their busy schedules to participate.

3. Task

There are five important exchanges related to this currency type: new resources, challenges, organizational support, getting something more quickly, and information. When we can realize that we don't have enough people working on our projects, we value new resources. When we go to our sponsor to fund those resources, we value organizational support. What do our sponsors get in exchange? A well-managed project! When we are easily bored with routine tasks, we usually value challenges. Those who ascribe to information being power might exchange information. On the above project, Elizabeth was able to get an expert to move from another state because the project would allow her to apply her expertise on a new software development tool and help her reputation and credibility by bringing new technology to the organization.

4. Relationship

There are three important exchanges related to this currency type: acceptance/inclusion, understanding, and personal support. We have found this to be an important currency when acquiring team members to work on a project. When the team is known to support each other; when they welcome and accept new team members; when there is a feeling of inclusion; when everyone is willing to pick up another's tasks when needed; and when we value relationships, it is far easier to acquire and keep resources. Those who understand that sharing information is power probably value the relationship currency. Elizabeth worked at a large financial institution that was very competitive and not a collaborative environment. They rarely socialized. They usually ate lunch alone at their desks. There was a picture of a group of turkeys with the words "Staff" printed at the top. Needless to say, no one felt supported or particularly close to each other. Elizabeth worked at another financial institution where the team was collaborative, self-directed, and close. In the first instance, it was hard to get cooperation; in the second, it was easy.

5. Personal

There are four important exchanges related to this currency type: gratitude, ownership/involvement, self-concept, and comfort. When we want to provide our support to those we know will appreciate it, we value gratitude. When we want to make a significant contribution to our organizations, we value ownership. When we work on a project because it reinforces our values or commitment to the organization, we value self-concept.

Table 3 provides a project example for each of the five currency types.

Currency	Key Concepts	Example
Inspirational	Vision and moral/ethical correctness, excellence	You'll get to work on a project that is essential to the success of this organization. And we need your particular set of skills to get this project in on time and within budget. This is a chance for you to use your skills to really help the organization.
Position	Recognition, visibility, reputation, importance, contacts	This is a chance for you to work on an important, large project. You've done a great job producing reports, but not too many people are aware of the great work you do. This project will give you the visibility you need to advance in this company and will broaden your reputation for doing great work. There are some important people involved on this project, and it will give you a chance to work with them.
Task	Resources, assistance, organizational support, rapid response	We really need your help defining the requirements for the new system. Were you aware that the new system will streamline your process? What used to take two hours will now take less than an hour. The project sponsor will provide resources to help out so that you can participate on this project.
	Challenges	We really need your technical expertise on this project. As you may have heard, we're implementing a new technical architecture. Working on this project will provide you with a chance to learn new skills.
	Information	We would love to have you on a new company-wide task force that's forming. It will be a chance for you to interview top executives and learn their thinking on the new product our company will be offering next year.

Currency	Key Concepts	Example
Relationship	Acceptance, understanding, personal support	We hope you'll be able to work on our team. We need your skills. We understand that you need to take some personal time off. That won't be a problem. We help each other out whenever there's a need. It's a great team!
Personal	Gratitude	We really appreciate your working overtime to meet our deadline. We have discussed the situation with our sponsor. She was unaware of the huge effort it is taking to bring the project in on time, and she specifically asked for your email so she could personally thank you.
	Ownership, self-concept	This is a very important, large project. The end product is something senior management has been wanting for years. We finally have the technology to support it. We need your help. Your knowledge of the business is crucial to the project's success. Your help on this project will directly benefit the organization. You have mentioned many times that it is important for you to make an impact on the organizations where you work. This is your chance to do so here.
	Comfort	Good news! We don't have to move to the 17th floor. If you agree to work on the project, you can stay right here with us.

TABLE 3: Five Currency Types Examples

Empowerment

We often hear the phrase "you are empowered" or "I empower you to...." If I empower you, I am authorizing you to act. That is, I am giving you the authority to act. But how can I realistically give you that authority? We know that project sponsors initiate projects with a project charter that provides the project manager with the "authority to apply resources to project activities."[10] But does that mean that we are truly empowered?

We wonder how one person can empower another. How can one person give another person power—the ability to influence? Again, we can give people authority, but that does not necessary lead to empowerment. We ran across one definition of business empowerment that speaks to this contradiction. That definition is "having the information, resources, and authority to make meaningful choices. A corporate head who delegates authority provides empowerment to division and department heads. "[11] We question whether empowerment can really be delegated. The implication, of course, is that without the authority, according to this definition, one cannot be empowered. We do not believe that.

A definition more to our liking comes from Vadim Kotelnikov, founder of the Ten3 Business e-Coach website,[12] which distinguishes between delegation and empowerment. With delegation comes authority and responsibility. The difficulty with delegation is that not everyone has the ability, motivation, and/or understanding to take on the assigned responsibility. An empowered work environment replaces delegation with empowerment and responsibilities with ownership.

It's a common assumption that if we are empowered, it is because of our own attitudes and perceptions, not someone else's. That is, it is triggered internally, unlike delegation, which is more externally triggered. Elizabeth worked in one organization that was not empowering, where everyone walked fast and bent forward at the waist. The image of puppets being pulled forward by an invisible hand comes to mind.

> *"Because information-sharing and collaboration were not highly regarded, I mistakenly concluded that I had to conform to this hierarchical, competitive culture. I felt completely un-empowered. I took orders rather than recommending solutions. And I was pretty miserable."*

Even though some employees can feel empowered in a non-empowering environment, most people need a corporate culture that supports collaboration. The website, "Tao of Employee Empowerment,"[13] lists the Yin and Yang or Receiving and Giving "Do"s of employee empowerment.[14]

Organizations can inspire, set high but realistic goals, encourage collaboration, discourage competition, encourage information-sharing, and do many of the things that build trust, which we will detail in the next chapter. Such a culture encourages employees to work together to recommend solutions, to produce high-quality work, and to take not only ownership of their work, but pride in producing outstanding results. These are truly empowering organizations.

Social Media

Social media provides a way to communicate using technology and the web. There are many different types of social media: Facebook for connecting to friends and family, LinkedIn for business connections and discussions, Twitter for serving as a microblog, YouTube for posting and viewing videos, wikis for information-sharing, virtual Internet games, product reviews, and more. There is a plethora of stories about how social media can influence outcomes. Most presidential campaigns in the United States use social media. But exactly how much influence they exert has not been proven. And we all know that the Arab Spring of 2011 is an example of changed outcomes and overthrown governments. Most people believe that use of social media was one of several contributing factors.

More and more companies are using social media to attempt to influence the products we buy. In his blog on market influencing, Michael Wu distinguishes between the influencer and the target. He suggests that there are two key and six sub-factors to take into consideration:[15]

- Credibility of the influencer, which he defines as domain expertise and enough bandwidth to influence through social media.
- The target's likelihood of being influenced.
- The relevance of the influencer's message to the target
- Timing of that message.
- Alignment of the social media channels (both need to be using the same ones).
- Confidence, or how much trust the target has in the influencer.

These factors apply equally to how we influence successfully on projects. Using Wu's paradigm, in all influencing transactions, there are influencers and targets. We'll talk more about how to prepare for these types of transactions in Chapter Four.

When using social media, we need to avoid the temptation to think that our tweets, our blogs, and our discussion entries are not only reaching our targets, but influencing them.

In addition, social media can be seductive. It can zap our time and energy. The editor of Social Media Influence, Matthew

Yoemans, states in his blog that "so much social media marketing remains stuck in a digital popularity contest that seeks to game customers simply to amass the quantity of fans and customers that satisfy a measurable metric...hopefully brands will move away from judging social media success through manufactured, meaningless social media popularity contests."[16]

More and more consumers are turning to social media to resolve their individual issues. And many companies ("brands") are responding to tweets "in order to maintain their reputations and sustain important customer relationships."[17] The same can be said for influencing on projects.

To summarize, it's easy to imagine that if others vote to "like" our articles, blog, and discussion comments, or if we have hundreds of Twitter followers, that we're effectively influencing. The use of social media can have both positive and negative consequences. The outcome of the Arab Spring may have different effects than the reformers expected because the latter didn't have the wherewithal to influence the implementation of the reforms.

The Trusted Advisor

Earlier in this chapter, we discussed Yuki and Tracy's influence tactics. One of those tactics is consultation, which, in a nutshell, consists of developing findings and presenting recommendations. It involves asking questions to find out the current situation, sometimes known as the "as-is," analyzing the situation, and developing recommendations for improvements.

TIP

The trusted advisor is really a management consultant, providing advice to those with authority.

In other words, we can influence others by being management consultants. Much of the mechanics for consultation are discussed in Chapters 6 and 7.

The trusted advisor is really a management consultant, providing advice to those with authority. The trusted advisor has to integrate the three components of the Influencing Formula. That is, trusted advisors need to build trust, be prepared, and act with courage. In this chapter, we introduce some of the challenges that the trusted advisor faces and provide tips for handling those challenges.

In the project world, trusted advisors can be any of the following:

- Project managers who need to advise sponsors, explaining project constraints, and recommending courses of action to the sponsor.
- Business analysts who need to advise the business owner, SMEs, testers, developers—anyone on the project team, including the project manager—when advice is needed related to the end product or solution.
- Team members who need to advise the project manager, business analyst, and other team members relating to risk, technical approaches and issues, project status, etc.

Tips for the Trusted Advisor

1. Provide advice, and remember that business decisions are always made by the business.

Trusted advisors do not make business decisions. They recommend solutions. We have always evangelized about the importance of sponsors and business owners making business decisions. Recently we had a conversation with a project manager who said that he viewed his role as making all decisions relevant to "his" project. When questioned about the types of decisions he made, he emphasized that he expected to have the level of freedom to make any decision that moved the project forward.

The conversation went something like this:

> **Us:** Who should make business decisions?

> **Him:** If I need those decisions made, I want the freedom to make them.

> **Us:** What is the role of the project sponsor?

> **Him (all too quickly)**: To approve the project.

> **Us:** What does that mean to you?

> **Him:** That he approves the project and authorizes me to make all the decisions affecting the project.

> **Us:** And if the sponsor made the decisions that related to the business?

> **Him**: We'd have a conversation about micromanagement.

TIP

1. Provide advice. Business decisions are always made by the business.

2. Do your homework. Saying "I'll get back to you" isn't good enough.

3. Take time to be thorough. It's worth every minute.

We thought about the myriad of decisions we make daily about running our business. As sponsors and business owners, we would not abdicate our responsibility nor would we put ourselves in a position to be accountable for someone else making those decisions for us. If we lay out the money to complete projects, we want to be sure we approve the decisions being made.

We also thought about the innumerable decisions we made as homeowners when our house was built. There is no way we would have left those decisions to the builder (i.e., the project manager). Why, we wonder, would any sponsor of any project want to abdicate control of the decisions to the project manager? Sponsors, after all, have a responsibility to the organization to deliver products and services that help organizations reach their goals. Why would they want to have anyone else make those decisions? The project manager has a lot to answer for. Business decisions just don't happen to be among them.

In their book, *The Trusted Advisor*, Maister, Green, and Galford list 22 traits of an effective trusted advisor, from the perspective of the person receiving the advice.[18] Among them are these:

Trusted advisors:

> "Help us [business owners] think things through (it's our decision)."

> "Don't substitute their judgment for ours."

> "Give us options, increase our understanding of those options, give us their recommendations, and let us choose."[19]

As business owners and sponsors, we are in complete agreement. Here is our perspective on these three traits:

- *Help us think things through.* We expect the trusted advisor to ask us good, insightful questions and not leading questions. We are not looking for trusted advisors to promote their personal agendas couched in questions; agreeing with a solution that has been presented is not the same thing as making our own decisions. If presented with solutions in the form of questions (e.g., "What do you think about..." or "would you consider..."), we need to make sure we all understand what problem that solution will solve. Leading questions, like those cited above, do not help us think things through. We want questions to get us out of the emotion of the moment and help us clarify our thoughts and our feelings so that our actions are aligned with our goals. Remember that ultimately it is the sponsor, not the trusted advisor, who has to live with those decisions.

- *Don't substitute your judgment for ours.* Throughout the years we've owned our company, we've dealt with innumerable consultants who have provided solutions without first making a business case. They have come in with lots of recommendations but no clarity on what problems those recommendations were solving. For example, a consultant recommended a new reporting structure without discussing what was wrong with the existing structure. Another badgered us into interviewing and then hiring someone who we didn't think would fit into our culture, providing numerous reasons why we were wrong and they were right in the judgment of this candidate. We caved and hired someone who lasted less than six months. To have relied on their judgment and given in to their relentless pressure was a big mistake in judgment on our part!

- *Give us options and let us choose.* These are golden words to a sponsor or business owner. As sponsors, the last thing we want is to be bullied with the term "micromanagement," which is the club some team members use from time to time to avoid tracking their time or to make decisions inappropriate for their role. We want your advice, but we want to choose what we know to be best for our organization. Feel free to point out the risks of our decisions, but never take away our choice.

2. Do your homework. Saying "I'll get back to you" is not good enough.

In later chapters, we will discuss the importance of preparation to contribute to influencing. There are many aspects to being prepared, including asking good questions to understand business problems, analyzing those problems, and recommending solutions. As trusted advisors, we need to be prepared to offer advice. We need to ask a great deal of questions, listen actively to all the responses, synthesize those responses, and provide advice.

There will be times, however, when we'll be asked for advice, and we need to be prepared to provide it. That is, the trusted advisor needs to anticipate questions from the business owner or sponsor, because when trusted advisors are asked, they actually need to give advice. Anticipating questions is what we do when we interview for a job. We think of all the possible questions that might be asked of us and prepare our responses. As trusted advisors, we are similarly prepared to answer questions that arise.

Sure, we may not be able to answer all questions. However, the preparation of answers to the questions we've anticipated provides us context so that we are not caught completely off guard. When possible, we want to avoid the excuse "I don't know the answer. I'll have to get back to you on that one." Such a response is better than lying, but it's usually not good enough. Imagine if every time we asked our doctors, lawyers, or financial advisors for advice they said, "I'm sorry I don't know. I'll have to get back to you on that," rather than providing options, risks, benefits, and recommendations.

Early in his career, Richard learned about anticipating questions the hard way by being surprised in an important presentation.

"I was presenting a business case to get funding for a new training project. It contained a great deal of 'evidence' I had compiled about

why our previous training program had improved the performance of the people receiving the training. Near the end of the presentation, a Senior Vice President asked 'I can see that the performance certainly improved. But, how do you know that it wasn't simply because we hired a higher caliber of employee and not your training program?' I was totally unprepared for that kind of question! Unfortunately I had to say 'I'll get back to you' and did not feel very influential."

3. Take the time to be thorough. It's worth every minute.

Trusted advisors are well-prepared, as we keep emphasizing. Some of that preparation means that we need to understand the impact of our recommendations to the business, to technology, and to the project.

- **Business impacts** - In order to understand business impacts, we need to understand the business. There is no substitute for spending time with the business, completing their processes, and using their automated systems. That experience not only helps us understand how our recommendations actually affect the daily lives of our stakeholders but also helps build relationships with the end-users. Importantly, spending time with stakeholders also provides the context we need to ask questions and make recommendations.

- **Technical impacts** - We provide the most value when we can discuss the impact of our recommendations to the technical environment. Some of those impacts we need to address are impacts to system and user interfaces, impacts to the databases (e.g., when purchasing commercial software), impacts to programs that pull and push information from the databases, and impacts to processing time to name a few. Trusted advisors need to understand just enough of the technical environment to explain in business terms how the technology will affect the business and, at a high level, how big the impacts are.

- **Project impacts -** Whether or not our recommendation is part of an initiative, program, portfolio, or specific project, we need to understand how it will affect the organization, what the most effective way to break the effort into projects is, and whether or not it is worthwhile.

- **Dependencies -** Most business executives know their priorities—what will provide the maximum benefit to the organization. Harder to know, however, are those pesky dependencies. As trusted advisors, we need to explain in business terms why certain things (tasks, requirements, projects, initiatives, etc.) need to be completed before others can be started.

The bottom line is that we need to present thorough recommendations. Future chapters detail how to be prepared so that we build a reputation for providing sound, well-analyzed advice.

Whose Advice Can Be Trusted?

Not everyone is ready to be a trusted advisor. It is easy to assume one is a trusted advisor prematurely, as Elizabeth recalls.

"I remember as a management consultant making recommendations to executives, thinking that I was a trusted advisor. To be sure, I was viewed as prepared and competent, a good presenter, articulate, and capable of learning quickly.

"But, I was not viewed as a trusted advisor. I was straight out of school and had few experiences that would provide me enough business context to be able to abstract situational issues and apply them to new situations.

"In addition, I had never failed at anything I tried, and although I had no idea at the time, I hadn't failed because my experience was too limited. I hadn't done anything significant enough to fail at it. And failure is such a great teacher!"

Many of us think that we can be trusted, pride ourselves on being thorough, and know we have the courage of our convictions. But how can you tell whether or not you have the experience to truly be a trusted advisor? Here are ten self-assessment questions to ask to confirm that you are ready to be a trusted advisor:

1. What have I learned from projects that have not succeeded (use any criteria for success)?
2. How do I keep informed of developments in my organization and industry?
3. How much do I enjoy immersing myself in detail in order to cover my bases and be credible?
4. Which are the areas of trust building that I exceed at? Which do I need to work on?
5. How many ways do I typically bust trust?
6. How have I handled the times when I have broken trust?
7. How often are my ideas and recommendations accepted?
8. How do I influence others to accept my ideas?
9. How comfortable am I expressing ideas that disagree with those in authority?
10. When I express those ideas, what style do I use?

"Trust one who has been through it."

THE AENEID, VIRGIL, 70 BC-19 BC

🖉 *Summary*

In this chapter, we have:

- Looked at some barriers to influencing, which we will explore further in future chapters.
- Presented eight approaches that we can take when we want to influence: rational persuasion, inspirational appeal, personal appeal, consultation, coalitions, ingratiation, relentless pressure, and reciprocity/exchange.
- Discussed how each of these approaches affects how we think, feel, and act and which demonstrate true leadership.
- Presented Bradford and Cohen's influence model containing five currency types of inspiration: position, task, personal, and relationship.
- Provided a project example of each.
- Explored the nature of empowerment and how it is taken rather than given.
- Discussed the ways social media works to influence companies and projects.
- Introduced the topic of the trusted advisor, providing three tips for being successful in that role.

1. G. Yuki and J.B. Tracy. "Consequences of influence tactics used with subordinates, peers, and the boss." *Journal of Applied Psychology*, (1992): 77, 525-535.

2   Allan R. Cohen & David L. Bradford. *Influence Without Authority*, 2nd ed. Hoboken, New Jersey: Wiley, 2005.

3   Chris Argyris, presented in Peter Senge et al.'s book *The Fifth Dimension Fieldbook: The Art and Practice of the Learning Organization*, 2004, accessed December 20, 2011, http://www.systems-thinking.org/loi/loi.htm.

4   David H. Maister, et al., *The Trusted Advisor*. New York: Simon & Schuster, 2000.

5   Cohen and Bradford. *The Influence Model: Using Reciprocity and Exchange to Get What You Need*, accessed August 20, 2012, http://influencewithoutauthority.com/files/influence_article_j_org_excellence.pdf.

6   G. Yuki and J.B. Tracy. "Consequences of influence tactics used with subordinates, peers, and the boss." *Journal of Applied Psychology*, (1992): 77, 525-535.

7   Dr. Dr. Gustavo Grodnitzky. Insights & Ideas from Gustavo Grodnitzky, Issue 9, Sept. 2004. Rational Persuasion Part II of IX, accessed December 02, 2011, http://www.drgustavo.com/LTP/Issue09.pdf.

8   Wikiquote. *Chinese proverbs*, accessed July 24, 2012, http://en.wikiquote.org/wiki/Chinese_proverbs.

9   Cohen and Bradford. *The Influence Model: Using Reciprocity and Exchange to Get What You Need*, accessed December 09, 2011, http://influencewithoutauthority.com/files/influence_article_j_org_excellence.pdf.

10 Project Management Institute. *A Guide to the Project Management Body of Knowledge (PMBOK® Guide)*, 4th ed. Appendix G5, (Newtown Square PA: Project Management Inst, 2008), Section 4.1.

11 YourDictionary.com, accessed December 22, 2011, http://business.yourdictionary.com/empowerment.

12 Vadim Kotelnikov. "Employee Empowerment: Harvesting the Creative and Emotional Power of All Your People." *Ten3 Business e-Coach*, accessed December 22, 2011, http://www.1000ventures.com/business_guide/crosscuttings/employee_empowerment.html.

13 Jane Smith. "Empowerment vs. Delegation." *Ten3 Business e-Coach*, accessed August 20, 2012, http://www.1000ventures.com/business_guide/crosscuttings/empowerment_vs_delegation.html.

14 YourDictionary.com, accessed December 22, 2011, http://business.yourdictionary.com/empowerment.

15 Michael Wu Ph.d. "*The 6 factors of Social Media Influence: Influence Analytics 1.*"Lithium, accessed January 04, 2012, http://lithosphere.lithium.com/t5/Building-Community-the-Platform/The-6-Factors-of-Social-Media-Influence-Influence-Analytics-1/ba-p/5708.

16 Matthew Yoemans (Editor at Large). "Getting over the need to be Liked."*Social Media Influence*, accessed January 04, 2012, http://socialmediainfluence.com/2011/12/29/getting-over-the-need-to-be-liked/.

17   Berhnard Warner. *"The amazingly gratifying angry customer service Tweet."* Social Media Influence, accessed January 04, 2012, http://socialmediainfluence.com/2011/10/26/the-amazingly-gratifying-angry-customer-service-tweet/#comments.

18   David H. Maister, et al., *The Trusted Advisor.* New York: Simon & Schuster, 2000.

19   Chris Argyris, Robert Putnam and Diana McLain Smith. *Action Science: Concepts, Methods and Skills for Research and Intervention.* (San Francisco CA: Jossey-Bass, 1985).

03 Building Trust

"Trust starts with truth and ends with truth."

SANTOSH KALWAR
CONTEMPORARY WRITER

K. O'Hara said that "trust is the big issue of the 21st century."[1] As recently as 2005, trust was not commonly discussed. Our company included the subject of trust as part of business analysis and project management training program because we have always thought that trust is necessary to eliciting complete requirements and building an effective team.

However, the project management and business analysis disciplines largely ignored such discussion. Today trust is, if not the biggest issue, certainly a big one. Not only are there innumerable presentations, white papers, and books about trust, it is hard to turn on the television or radio without hearing about trust related to sports, politics, education, parenting, and other subjects. Several factors have turned trust into this important topic, among them:

1. Global projects

Such efforts have encouraged collaboration. Reliance on virtual, self-directed teams requires trust-based relationships.

2. Speed

The need to complete work more quickly than ever before has encouraged a team-based approach of sharing information. It also discouraged a hierarchical organizational structure, which slows communication, thereby delaying the project. In software development, Agile methods are widely used. Such methods are based on collaboration and trusting a self-directed team to get the job done.

In the mid-1990s, Elizabeth worked for an organization whose directive from the top was to get the work done quickly. As Tom Peters said, "Speed is Life: Go Fast or Go Broke"[2]

"Ours was a culture of collaboration. However, one of the other divisions had a culture that was more political in nature. The in-fighting and backstabbing made it almost impossible to elicit requirements during requirements workshops, and projects took far longer."

Background

Today there is a body of literature on the subject of trust, including eBooks, articles, and journals. Some that we found helpful include:

- Stephen M. R. Covey's *The Speed of Trust* is practical and informative.[3] The paradigm of the four cores of credibility is powerful. We will discuss this concept in more detail later in this chapter.

- K. O'Hara, (2004). *Trust: From Socrates to Spin*. Cambridge: Icon Books Ltd.

- Bradford and Cohen's *Influence Without Authority* and their Influence Model based on reciprocity and exchange. The concept of exchange has been gaining acceptance in the last several years. We will discuss the concept of exchange and the currencies that are used for exchange in the business environment later in the chapter.

- Grudzewski's (et. al). article, *Trust Management – The New Way in the Information Age,* which discusses the reasons why organizations need to focus strategically on trust.

- Maister, Green, and Galford's book titled *The Trusted Advisor*[4] (2000). It applies to all industries. Although much of its focus is from the perspective of an outside consultant providing services to a client, there is a great deal of useful information contained in this small, easy-to-read book. One of the authors, Charles Green, has a newsletter, called *Trusted Advisor*,[5] with articles, blogs, videos, and tips.

- Dennis Reina and Michelle Reina created the Trust and Betrayal Model, which provides seven steps for restoring trust.[6]

Defining Trust

When we think about trust, we think of it in a variety of different ways as it applies to the many areas in our lives. To cite just a few examples, we *trust* in something so that when:

- We lean against a wall or sit on a chair, it won't collapse.
- The gas tank in the car says "full," we won't run out of gas.
- We visit our doctors, they have the education and experience to address our medical concerns.
- We send our children to school, the teachers have our children's best interests at heart.
- Our project team executes the project, they want both the organization and the project to succeed.

In other words, we trust both people and objects.

In August 2007, an eight-lane freeway bridge over the Mississippi River in Minneapolis, Minnesota, USA, collapsed, killing 13 people and injuring 145. The bridge simply disappeared from under them during rush hour traffic. Five years later one of the survivors spoke about her experience. She said that now, five years after the collapse, she still has fears about bridges collapsing under her. When she is in her car on a bridge, she has her finger on the window button in case the bridge collapses. When she is in an elevator she holds onto a railing in case it crashes to the ground. "It's just a thing I do now," she said.[7] In other words, her trust in objects that could fall has been broken.

Here are two definitions of trust:

1. "Trust is the confident reliance on someone when you are in a position of vulnerability."[8] [9] We like the words "confidence" and "reliance," which imply security and reliability. We also like the element of "vulnerability," which implies that we could get hurt if the person (for example, a project team member) or thing (our car that we need to get to work) proves untrustworthy.

2. "Reliance on the integrity, strength, ability, surety, etc., of a person or thing."[10] We like the words "reliance," as well as "integrity," which implies internal consistency (more later in the chapter), strength, because we don't trust people or things we perceive as weak, and "ability," which, as we'll discuss later in this chapter, is an important component of credibility.

Waves of Trust

In his book, *Speed of Trust*, Stephen M.R. Covey (son of the prolific Stephen R. Covey) discusses what he calls "waves of trust." Starting with self-trust, proceeding to relationship trust, moving through organizational trust, market trust, and finally societal trust, Covey discusses how trust ripples outwards through all aspects of one's life. *Table 4* clarifies these waves of trust, which are listed with a summary of key concepts and an example of how this concept applies to a project.

Wave	Key Concepts	Example
Self-Trust	Credibility in the eyes of others, who will only trust us if we are deemed credible. Credibility is comprised of our character and competence.	"It's possible no one will question where I got these benefit numbers from. But, it doesn't feel right to just guess, so I'll put in some overtime to research them."
Relationship Trust	Generating trust with others, based on consistent behavior.	"Paula talks a great line. But have you ever noticed that she says one thing when Management is in the room and another when she talks to her direct reports?"
Organizational Trust	Alignment of those we trust in an organization. Do we trust our team but not our management?	"Kyle asked me to work on this project. I'm concerned that it's his own pet project and that it's not aligned with the organization's business objectives."
Market Trust	An organization's reputation in the marketplace, its brand, and the amount of customer loyalty.	In 2011 General Motors surpassed Toyota in sales and market share, after falling behind in previous years. Toyota was plagued with recall issues. "Another reason for Toyota's decline is the recall of their products due to safety reasons."[11]

Wave	Key Concepts	Example
Societal Trust	Contribution and creating value for others.	In 2008 Bill Gates announced his transition from head of Microsoft to be able to spend more time with the Bill and Melinda Gates Foundation, whose mission is, among other things, to enhance healthcare and reduce extreme poverty.

TABLE 4: Examples of Covey's Waves of Trust

There is a critical relationship between credibility and trust. We cannot build trust if we are not perceived as credible. There are many aspects to credibility. There is the credibility related to our work, to our financial commitments, to keeping our promises. It is hard to establish credibility and easy to lose it. For example, we lose credibility when we do not complete work on time or when we promise to meet someone and call to cancel when something better comes up. We lose credibility when we:

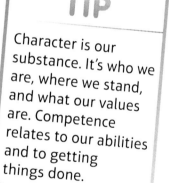

TIP

Character is our substance. It's who we are, where we stand, and what our values are. Competence relates to our abilities and to getting things done.

- Take out a loan and fail to make payments or when we sign up to attend a professional association meeting and fail to show up.

- Promise to attend our child's play or sporting event and have to stay late at work.

- Are given a project end-date and accept it without question, without developing a plan to get an idea of a reasonable end-date, and fail to meet that date. There are dozens of examples of how we lose credibility and others' willingness to trust us.

In his *Speed of Trust*, Covey breaks "credibility" into two categories: character and competence.

Character is our substance. It's who we are, where we stand, and what our values are.

Competence relates to our abilities and to getting things done.

Covey further breaks character and competence into the four cores of credibility. Character is comprised of Integrity and Intent; Competence is made up of Capabilities and Results. More details on each of the cores of credibility follow.

Figure 2 is a diagram showing this breakdown.

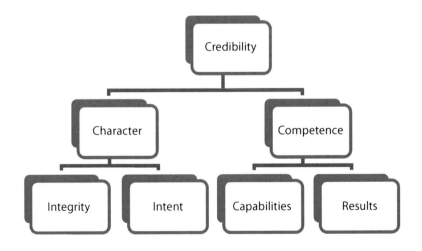

FIGURE 2: Covey's Four Cores of Credibility

Character

There was a time when noting someone's strength of character was the biggest compliment one could give another person. Calling a person a liar (reflection of a weak character) could result in a duel. Henry Clay, the statesman and politician (1777-1852), said, "Of all the properties which belong to honorable men, not one is so highly prized as that of character."[12]

"I hope I shall always have firmness and virtue enough to maintain, what I consider the most enviable of all titles, the character of an honest man."

GEORGE WASHINGTON

When talking about a character in technical terms, a character is a symbol. As related to trust, character is a symbol as well. It symbolizes who we are fundamentally, our essence if you will, and what we stand for. Abraham Lincoln (16th U.S. President) said, "Character is like a tree and reputation like its shadow. The shadow is what we think of it; the tree is the real thing."

Literary figures, such as Shakespeare's King Henry V, Jane Austen's Mr. Knightley (from *Emma*), and Harper Lee's Atticus Finch (*To Kill a Mockingbird*) are examples of people with strong character or substance. In literature, we also talk about character flaws. When protagonists overcome their flaws, there is growth and a positive outcome, as in Austen's *Emma*. The inability to overcome these flaws results in tragedy.

A tragic flaw (hamartia) is "a character defect that causes a downfall of the protagonist of a tragedy.[13] In an example from Shakespeare's *Othello*, Iago is Othello's trusted advisor. The latter trusts him and the advice he provides. It is commonly accepted that the evil Iago is able to bring about death and destruction by playing on the protagonist's (Othello) character defect: jealousy, a form of mistrust. It is ironic that Othello trusts Iago, whom he should not, and mistrusts his wife, Desdemona, whom he should. This mismatch of trust is his character defect and causes the unhappy outcome.[15]

> *"Watch your thoughts, for they become words. Watch your words, for they become actions. Watch your actions, for they become habits. Watch your habits, for they become character. Watch your character, for it becomes your destiny."*
>
> **UNKNOWN**

Of course, we all have character, and intuitively we understand the difference between good and bad, weak and strong character. When we lie, when we have our own agendas, and when we go along with the crowd, we demonstrate bad character at worst and weak character at best.

The Josephson Institute, Center for Business Ethics, describes six pillars of character.[15] These pillars combine several of the concepts related to Covey's Credibility, although there are additional aspects as well.

The six pillars include:

1. **Trustworthiness** - Being honest, reliable, having the courage to do the right thing, being loyal, and building a good reputation. Trustworthiness is one of the competencies cited in *A Guide to the Business Analysis Body of Knowledge* (BABOK® Guide)[16], a competency being something that supports business analysis but is needed in most other disciplines. Both PMI and IIBA require their certified practitioners sign a code of ethics as a pledge of trustworthiness.

2. **Respect** - Being tolerant and accepting of differences, dealing peacefully with disagreements.

3. **Responsibility** - Planning, preserving, considering consequences, setting a good example, and being accountable.

4. **Fairness** - Listening to others, being open-minded, and taking responsibility rather than blaming others.

5. **Caring** - Being kind and compassionate, expressing gratitude, expressing forgiveness.

6. **Citizenship** - Volunteering, cooperation, protecting the environment, obeying laws, being a concerned neighbor.

As noted earlier, Covey's Character has two components.

Integrity includes honesty, it includes authenticity, but is much more. It is having an internal moral compass and consistency. We often refer to someone who "walks the talk" as having integrity, which means their actions are consistent with their espoused beliefs.

People with integrity courageously stand for what they believe.

Covey discusses integrity as "congruence," as having "no gap between intent and behavior." We could have the best intentions in the world, but the way we act might cause a large gap between that good intent and have a bad effect on others.

Covey also includes humility as a component of integrity. We've all encountered arrogant people, and often we instinctively avoid them. We might not put this mistrust into words, though, and relating arrogance to lack of integrity provides an explanation for our aversion.

TIP

We could have the best intentions in the world, but the way we act might cause a large gap between that good intent and have a bad effect on others.

Covey also puts courage in the Integrity category. However, because we feel so strongly that courage is an essential ingredient in influencing, we will cover it as a separate chapter.

Integrity, of course, includes being honest. When we lie, when we cheat, when we omit, and when we deceive, we lack integrity. In an article entitled "Topics of Discussion: What Is Integrity,"[17] John Richardson describes integrity, acknowledging that most people think of integrity as honesty. However, his description of integrity is that of alignment of actions with values, thoughts, and feelings. He cites the example that when we are late for meetings or don't show up at all, we lack integrity. That seems like a stretch. However, when we think about accepting a meeting at a specific time as a commitment, then showing up late or not at all is an example of not meeting a commitment.

Richardson also notes that working on projects is an area that challenges his consistency and therefore his integrity. Projects always take longer than planned. In our training classes, we focus on bringing projects in on time, and "on time" means as promised. Yes, promised.

When working as a project manager, Elizabeth took this promise very seriously and learned it is more complicated than it may appear at first.

> *"As a project manager, I had a tendency to push the team to meet the deadline, because at a certain point in the project, usually after we had the detailed requirements, I made a commitment to bring the project in by the deadline our team had provided. In other words, missing a deadline was like breaking my promise and would reflect negatively on my character. What I failed to realize was that my perceived lack of concern for the team also reflected poorly on my integrity and therefore my character."*

Intent focuses on our motives and ensuring that they are transparent. It is about communicating our agenda so that everyone involved knows what they are. As Covey says, "declare your intent.[18]" Intent is related to integrity in that there needs to be consistency between our intentions and what others think our intentions are.

Elizabeth once worked as a project manager in an organization with many project managers.

> *"One day, in an off-hand comment, another project manager made a comment about 'the dumb users.' She added that she dutifully listened to the Subject Matter Experts' (SMEs') requirements, ignored everything they said, and proceeded with what she thought was best for them. She never told them that she ignored their requirements. She said that she understood better than they what they really needed. I remember being uncomfortable that her intentions were so lacking in transparency. Worse yet, this woman was highly esteemed in the organization, and I wondered if I would ever succeed in an environment that valued this kind of duplicitous behavior. I found both her motives and her lack of transparency profoundly troubling."*

In technology, intent is an abstract description of an operation to be performed.[19] As it relates to trust, intent is also a kind of description of behavior that will be performed. Some action will happen, and the intent describes the expected action or behavior.

The relation to integrity is described by Glenn Paskin, published in Dr. Wayne Dyer's newsletter.[20] "A caterpillar, a tiny acorn, an apple blossom all have intention built into them. That caterpillar becomes a butterfly, the acorn a giant oak tree, the apple blossom an apple. Intention doesn't err. The acorn never turns into a pumpkin! Every aspect of nature has intention built in."

In other words, there is complete consistency between what is supposed to happen and what actually does happen. Where there is inconsistency, there is bad intent and a lack of integrity, that is, of internal consistency.

Competence addresses our ability to get the job done. It is impossible to establish credibility if we are not viewed as competent. Competence is a combination of our abilities. It answers the question: "Do we have the wherewithal to get results, and if so, can we, and if so, do we?"

> **TIP**
>
> Competence addresses our ability to get the job done. It is impossible to establish credibility if we are not viewed as competent.

Capabilities are a combination of ingredients that make us useful to others, be they organizations, family, or friends. Capabilities might include such things as the skills we have developed, our knowledge and expertise, and our innate abilities.

An English major has the ability to be an English teacher, but the desire is separate from the ability. Someone might love to be a scientist, maybe a quantum physicist. Unfortunately, if that person is mathematically challenged, that career is not a possibility. One needs the capabilities to pursue such a career.

It is interesting to watch the varied capabilities of our grandsons blossom. While they all excel in sports, one is artistically creative, one has a passion for music, one is a whiz with numbers, etc.

TIP

Our credibility is based on our ability to get quality projects done on time.

Results How often do we hear the phrase "she has so much potential" or "he could really be good at that if he only tried." These people have capabilities but are not producing results. How many of us have thought that learning to play the piano is a great idea but have been less thrilled about practicing? Many project managers have the ability to be good project managers but could never deliver the project on time. Others delivered the project on time, but the results were filled with defects. Our credibility is based on our ability to get quality projects done on time.

In order to establish and maintain credibility, we need a combination of all four components.

We've known business analysts who had capabilities relating to analyzing requirements but who were clueless about building rapport with clients. Likewise, we've known project managers who could deliver projects on time but wreaked havoc with the team. An example is a boss who can be the nicest person in the world but lacks the courage to support us when we present our recommendations to the executive committee.

Ways to Build and Bust Trust

Building Trust

Trust usually takes time to develop. In addition, the farther away people are from each other, the harder it is to build trust. Building relationships on virtual teams, therefore, is more difficult than on teams that are colocated. We will provide more details on virtual teams later in the chapter. We may initially trust or not trust those involved on our projects based on past experience, personal filters, culture (organizational, geographical, and otherwise), and a wide variety of factors that can influence our judgments.

Business analysts and project managers don't always have time to let relationships develop, so here are some things that can be done to build trust quickly:

First, remember Covey's Four Cores of Credibility. Character and competence do matter. It is impossible to build trust without them. Most ways to build trust fall into either or both categories of Character or Competence. We developed our initial list of 15 ways to build trust in the late 1990s. We have been adding to it throughout the years as we encounter new experiences and information.

As you read the list below, think about whether these trust-building approaches relate more to character or competence and which of the four categories of the four cores they belong to.

Be honest. We all know the old adage that "honesty is the best policy." We know we should be truthful; that "honesty pays." We know that if we are always truthful, we will never have to remember what we've said. Lying is an assault on one's character, in particular on one's integrity. Nevertheless, we've heard that "all politicians tell lies."

Instead of holding politicians accountable, we accept their lies. Or we've heard someone criticizing another as being "honest to a fault." However, we don't think the fault is honesty but rather the style of the communication.

Be authentic. As Oscar Wilde quipped, "Be yourself; everyone else is already taken."[21] Authenticity happens when we are sincere, when we speak from our hearts, and when we are empathetic. Some politicians seem to have forgotten how important authenticity is. When asked by a reporter what he thought about the death of a colleague, a politician answered "no comment," leaving the impression that he had to be briefed by the party chair on an appropriate response. Although we need to keep Covey's style in mind when we speak from our hearts, we cannot be so afraid of offending others that we couch our words in a cloud of ambiguity.

Communicate early and openly. Or as some would suggest, early and often. It has been suggested that we can't over-communicate, but we don't agree. Have you ever gotten too many emails, even from well-intentioned individuals? Have you been double and triple booked for meetings because a well-intentioned associate wants to make sure you get the information? Our advice is to ask stakeholders about the frequency of communications, including meetings, and communicate according to their wishes. Open, transparent communication, however, is part of Intent, one of Covey's four cores of credibility.

Communicate bad news. When the project is behind schedule, when it needs more resources, or when lack of stakeholder participation is slowing the project, it is important for project managers and business analysts to

TIP

Establishing trust with key stakeholders is the best protection for communicating bad news.

address these issues with the sponsor and other appropriate team members. Communicating bad news takes courage. Establishing trust with key stakeholders is the best protection for communicating bad news.

Here are some tips to give you the courage needed to communicate bad news:

1. Be prepared. We have found that being prepared with information, such as the reason for delays and plans to get back on track, is a good way to gain the necessary courage to communicate bad news.

2. Set expectations early in the project that there may be delays, a need for additional resources, help in resolving conflict, etc. Ask for input on the preferred approach to escalating issues. Document your intent and understanding as part of your communications plan.

Acknowledge mistakes. Some organizations make it clear the minute you step in the door that mistakes are not tolerated. You can feel the atmosphere of intimidation and recrimination and hear it in the hallway conversations.

Acknowledging mistakes in such a culture is difficult and risky. However, the rewards are numerous. Taking full responsibility for mistakes helps develop a loyal, dedicated staff and is an effective antidote to blame.

> **TIP**
>
> Knowledge provides the context we need to ask good questions and make good decisions, which in turn will build not only our confidence but others' confidence in us.

Learn from mistakes. It's one thing to acknowledge mistakes; it's another to ensure that the same mistakes are not repeated. Holding lessons learned sessions, acknowledging and internalizing the lessons, documenting the results, and reviewing the previous lessons from similar situations provides confidence that the same mistakes will not be repeated.

Give credit where credit is due. Some of Elizabeth's prior bosses took her recommendations and put their own name on them. Then, when things went wrong, they passed the blame to her.

Make commitments. We have also known of bosses who never had to meet commitments because they never make any. Making commitments means taking a stand. It means being willing to be held accountable. It means taking a risk because many things can get in the way of meeting commitments once they are made. Making commitments does not guarantee that we will be able to meet them because there are too many unforeseen events that might prevent our ability to do so. However, verbalizing that proverbial line in the sand, knowing that it could get washed away, makes it more real and provides internal incentives for meeting them.

Meet commitments. We may not always be able to meet commitments, but once they are verbalized, we need to find creative ways to determine how to do so.

When we cannot, we need to communicate that we can't, why we are not able to, and when we can. If we keep missing our commitments, we will not be credible, and we don't want a pattern of making a commitment, not meeting it, setting a new date, and missing it again. The airlines found out about the psychological effect of promising unrealistic arrival times. Now they plan delays into the schedule.

There is no reason to "pad" the estimate for each task. Instead, add contingency for expected delays, such as training new team members, researching change requests, and technology issues.

Be competent within the domain of expertise. We have addressed the need for competence. However, we cannot be competent in everything. We need to know our organization, our industry, our projects, our stakeholders, and our profession. This knowledge provides the context we need to ask good questions and make good decisions, which in turn will build not only our confidence but others' confidence in us.

Respect the domain expertise of others. The subject matter experts (SMEs) assigned to our projects, whether business or technical, have been assigned for their expertise. When we talk about "dumb users," or "arrogant IT," we demean the others and risk the relationship. When we step on others' expertise by showing off our knowledge of their domain, we also demean the person's expertise and risk a ruined relationship. We have known technical experts to argue with business experts about business solutions. We have known business analysts to argue with technical experts about program code. Sponsors have been known to demand technical solutions. Each of these instances shows lack of respect for the expertise of the other parties.

Plan/anticipate/monitor/control. Developing a comprehensive plan shows that we've done our homework and goes a long way to build trust. It shows that we're willing to spend the time to be thorough.

Anticipating risks and creating risk response plans provides confidence that, should a risk event occur, the team has a way to mitigate it. Monitoring provides confidence that the plans that were developed will be reviewed, that actuals will be compared to the plan, and that variances will be appropriately

> **TIP**
>
> Anticipating risks and creating risk response plans provides confidence that, should a risk event occur, the team has a way to mitigate it.

handled. Controlling provides confidence that adjustments will be made to correct the plan. When our stakeholders know that we take the time to plan the tasks, capture the actuals, and adjust the plan, they are more likely to trust our commitments.

Provide frequent updates, to be determined by the stakeholders. Providing status updates is a key factor in building trust. Communicating at regular intervals, to be determined by the stakeholders themselves, lets them know that you have the project, or at least your part of the project, under control. The stakeholders will have different ideas about what is enough and what is too much. Elizabeth has seen a wide range of ideas from different bosses.

> "I once had a boss who, when I went into his office to make him aware of an issue, told me to just send him an email. Another boss in the same organization, when I sent him an email, told me he preferred face-to-face communications. 'What's the matter,' he asked, 'are you mad at me or something? Why don't you come see me?' In either case, it was important to keep the boss informed, but each had a different way they wanted to hear from me."

Respect, value, and accept others and value their input. We build trust by being inclusive. When we listen to what others have to say, acknowledge their ideas even when we disagree, have open discussions, and seek out people who disagree with us and who are different from us, we build trust and loyalty.

Acknowledge others' contributions. Even when we disagree, we need to genuinely appreciate others' contributions. A dominating participant can shut down discussion. Meetings and workshops will have lowered participation when a facilitator disagrees with a participant rather than remaining neutral. Better to encourage everyone's input and find ways to reach consensus when disagreements occur.

Be "present." When talking to someone who is playing with a cell phone or talking to someone who interrupts the conversation to pick up the phone, or seems distracted in any way, many people blame themselves. They worry they are simply boring or wasting this person's time. Some will even fear they are not good enough. All these worries are soon replaced with annoyance at the lack of respect. For people to trust us, we need to give them our attention. We need to listen to them and hear them. We need to focus on them and their needs.

Meet deadlines. Few things destroy trust among project team members more than having someone not meet deadlines. When other team members count on us to get our job done and we don't, we let people down. We become a roadblock that prevents them from completing their tasks. The project is delayed. The sponsor becomes unhappy. Morale suffers.

Communicate when you can't. However, we cannot always meet our deadlines. Things happen on projects that get in the way of getting our tasks completed. As important as it is to complete our work on time, it is equally important to recognize that, when problems arise, we need to communicate that we cannot.

Creating a communications plan sets communications expectations, including who to notify when we fall behind and at what point to so communicate. Let's say, for example, that for one week a team member on our project falls behind schedule due to unique, unforeseen circumstances that are not apt to happen again and will not cause further delays. Do we communicate this delay? And if so, to whom? A communication plan

> **TIP**
>
> As important as it is to complete our work on time, it is equally important to recognize that, when problems arise, we need to communicate that we cannot.

will provide such guidance. In our example, the team member might notify the project manager, but the project manager might decide not to communicate this specific delay to the sponsor.

Keeping on top of these types of communications challenges is one of the most challenging but important responsibilities of the project manager. Without a plan, communication is apt to take longer and be less effective.

Act consistently. Consistency is at the heart of integrity, as we saw in Covey's paradigm above. When our behavior is inconsistent, those interacting with us cannot predict our behavior. When they don't know how we will react, particularly to bad news, they might be afraid to approach us. As project professionals, we need information, sometimes in very short time frames, so we need people to be willing to discuss issues with us in an open way. Acting consistently is a key to getting this information we need so that we can take the required action.

Richard had a boss who was highly inconsistent:

> *"It seemed unpredictable to me which side would come out, the one who was happy with my work, or the one who was critical and 'nit-picked' the details of what I did. It was uncomfortable interacting with him and hard for me to trust him, since I thought my work was more consistent than that."*

Protect your good reputation. A good reputation is a mark of both character and competence. Having a good reputation relating to our character is necessary but not sufficient. The team may trust our character but not our competence. If we are not viewed as competent, however, our team will not trust us.

If we usually miss our deadlines and communicate appropriately, we will contribute to our reputation relating to honesty. However, if we usually miss our deadlines, even if we communicate that we have done so, we will develop a reputation for being incompetent, and therefore untrustworthy. Once we establish a good reputation, we need to work hard at protecting it. We need to be aware that others in the organization, for reasons that might be totally unrelated to us, might want to tarnish our reputation. We cannot always stop gossip, but if we protect our reputation, we can minimize its negative effects.

> *"A good reputation is more valuable than money."*
>
> **PUBILIUS SYRUS**

Take time and the initiative to learn new things. This advice addresses competence. When we take the time and show interest in learning new things, without delaying our projects, we build confidence in our abilities to handle new challenges.

Share information. Sharing information is a characteristic of transparency, which is one way to build trust. We used to say that "information is power." Now we say that sharing information is power. Why? Because when we withhold information, people work less effectively. More time is spent on the proverbial "grapevine," trying to find out what's happening on our team, in our area, and in our organization. When we withhold information, we find ourselves working alone or in silos, which requires more time to communicate—to send and receive our communications— as well as to process the information we receive. When we share information with others, information that is necessary for the team to do their job, we communicate that we have nothing to hide, so there is less time spent searching for information and spending time in idle speculation.

Communicate for the audience at hand. When we talk "techie" to business people, for example, or use idioms and slang to an audience more comfortable with a more formal language (particularly when speaking to people less familiar with our language), we run the risk of losing their attention and their trust. Elizabeth has learned this:

> "I remember interviewing members of an IT organization and feeling very foolish because I didn't understand their acronyms. I also felt more of an 'us' and 'them' atmosphere. They used language surrounded in mystique, and while that was interesting, it was also uncomfortable, and did nothing to build trust."

Use appropriate body language. We often hear that we need to use good body language. But what does "good" mean? It means appropriate to the situation at hand. If we are communicating during a formal presentation, our body language will be different than if we are communicating at home. If we are communicating with people from another culture, we need to understand their body language norms, such as distance between speaker and listener, use of eye contact, what nodding the head means, and so forth. Using inappropriate body language can destroy trust, as these unintentional faux pas can cause offense.

Discuss the project objectives openly. For example, if reducing headcount is a business objective and the project in question may contribute to meeting that objective, the project manager or analyst needs to communicate the possibility to the stakeholders if asked. Such a conversation can lead to one about the advantages to the employee of actively participating to help the organization meet its goals. Trust will not be built by avoiding the conversation or asking the stakeholders to discuss it with their bosses. Confronting the issue in a straightforward way requires courage but builds trust.

Encourage laughter. If you Google the question, "Can laughter build trust?" you will find many studies about the correlation between laughter and trust. Having fun in meetings and laughing appropriately (not hurtfully) even when the team is under pressure builds a sense of team solidarity and a desire to work together towards the desired project outcome.

Define clear roles and responsibilities. When not defined, tasks overlap and, even more commonly, fall through the cracks, which invariably leads to finger-pointing, blame, and lowered morale. Clear definition helps prevent territorial squabbling and helps reduce the chance of misunderstanding and the resulting project delays.

Trust usually takes time to develop. We may initially trust or distrust those involved on our projects based on past experience, personal filters, culture (organizational, geographical, and otherwise), and a wide variety of factors that can influence our judgments. Analysts and project managers don't always have time to let relationships develop, so many of the items we presented are intended to build trust quickly.

TIP

- Start with "electronic courtship."
- Clarify goals, roles, and responsibilities.
- Be positive and enthusiastic!

Virtual Teams

A virtual team consists of individuals who are not physically colocated. These individuals might work in different buildings, states, or countries. Does building trust look different for virtual teams? To some extent yes, to some extent no.

Virtual teams with the highest levels of trust tend to share three traits. They:

- *Start with "electronic courtship."* That is, they begin their interactions by introducing themselves and providing some personal background before focusing on the work at hand. This is called "electronic courtship."

- *Clarify goals, roles, and responsibilities.* As important as it is to clarify roles, responsibilities, and accountabilities on a colocated team, it is even more so for a virtual team.

- *Are consistently positive and enthusiastic* in all of their messages. There will be issues on the project that would be difficult to resolve with a colocated team but are even harder when the team is geographically dispersed. However, it is much easier to get through the difficulties and provide support to each other when all members are positive about their participation on the project and the team.

The most successful virtual teams are self-organizing, which means that all team members:

- *Are more concerned with getting the job done* than in the process for completing tasks. Virtual teams cannot be bogged down in bureaucracy or by having to follow a burdensome methodology. They need to focus on getting the job done, not the process for doing so.

- *Allow leaders to emerge,* rather than choose leaders. Many teams, virtual teams in particular, seem to function best when a leader emerges rather than being appointed. Anyone with leadership skills can lead the team. In the last chapter, we talked about leadership, or personal power. Even when someone has authority, or positional power, it does not mean that he or she is the most effective leader. Teams working on Agile projects know that anyone on the team can be the leader. It is not necessarily the project manager who can best get the team motivated and moving in the right direction. Although it might be, it does not need to be.

- *Pitch in* and help the team as needed. In our organization, account managers support each other when another account manager is on vacation, maternity leave, or gone for personal reasons. They follow up with clients, resolve client issues, and schedule appointments and classes, all without any expectation of financial gain. Each helps the others out. On a virtual team, such support is critical because on a virtual team it's easier to "disappear." That is, when we are dispersed, we cannot track someone down at their desk. We cannot meet with them face-to-face to encourage active participation. Unless we willingly help each other out, we risk having the project fall behind.

- *Willingly engage in project management* activities. For example, team members understand the importance of tracking their actuals against plan and reporting their status. They understand that project management tools and techniques serve to enhance team communications.

Successful virtual teams:

- Get the job done.
- Allow leaders to emerge.
- Pitch in and help.
- Plan and track their time.
- Give and receive feedback.
- Create communications ground rules.
- Provide frequent updates.
- Display concern for team members.
- Meet face-to-face.
- Take time off to get to know other team members.
- Are comfortable with technology.

- *Give feedback* intended to improve the content of each other's work. It is important for the team, once they have built trust among themselves, to feel comfortable getting and receiving feedback on their deliverables. Both giving and getting feedback is difficult under the best of circumstances. It is hard to have the courage to provide feedback. It is hard not to get defensive when receiving it. It is important for the format of the feedback to be positive, and words such as "the deliverable would be even better if it..." are less likely to put the receiving team member on the defensive.

- *Create communication protocol,* or ground rules, to address such things as:

  - How often each team member will provide updates.
  - How much time after an email or text is sent will lapse before the team member answers it.
  - How formal communications should be.
  - How frequently team members notify each other of their whereabouts and absences as promised.

- *Display concern for the well-being of team members.* This concern is expressed for both work and personal issues and is expressed as support and willingness to help out in any way that helps the team.

- *Meet face-to-face* at least once. All of us who have been on virtual teams know that it's easier to build relationships and trust after we have met someone face to face. Although there are some really sophisticated collaboration tools, it is still easier to build trust by meeting in person at least once.

- *Take time off to get to know other team members.* When we cannot meet fact-to-face, it is useful to set up a meeting whose sole purpose is personal. It is helpful to prepare for this meeting as we would with any other. That is, think about what you want to know and prepare questions relating to family, favorite or upcoming vacations, favorite books, music or movies, how they do or do not use social media, favorite activities, etc.

- *Use a variety of technology* and social media, such as Skype/ Facetime, texting, LinkedIn, email, phone conversations, etc.

Maintaining Trust Over Time

Once trust is established, it can lead the team members through project difficulties. However, trust is hard to build but easy to break. And once broken, it cannot easily be regained. The remainder of the chapter will discuss breaking and restoring trust.

Busting the trust of your project team, peers, and business stakeholders is pretty easy. As Sophocles said, "Trust dies, but mistrust blossoms."[22] There are lots of ways to destroy trust. For example, we might think of all the ways to build trust and then do the opposite, such as being dishonest, or lacking authenticity, or being unwilling to communicate bad news. What follows are ten additional ways to bust trust. There are, of course, many more. These are just a few of our favorite ways to bust trust.

1. **Gossip.** Gossiping is fun, right? It's great to be in the center of who knows what about everything and everyone. Some people use gossip as a currency. Feed me a juicy tidbit, and I'll give you two in return. So why does gossiping bust trust? If I tell you a piece of gossip about someone, do you really think I wouldn't tell others about you?

2. **Use humor inappropriately.** Have you ever joked around during a meeting or requirements workshop, making wise cracks or being sarcastic? Have you ever told the facilitator who was trying to enforce ground rules, "What's the matter? Don't you have a sense of humor?" We may pride ourselves on our cleverness, but others in the meeting might feel dismissed or that their ideas are being trivialized. It's a great way to ensure that the agenda stalls and that the meeting objectives are not reached. If you are the constant joker, join the club of trust busters.

3. **Be competitive.** When we are collaborative, value others' input, and are interested in a solution that meets the organizational goals and project objectives, we will probably not succeed in busting trust. But when we put our self-interest ahead of the team, when we don't listen to others' ideas, when, darn it, our way is the right way and we argue our position rather than listening actively to others, we have a good shot at busting trust.

4. **Withhold information.** Ah, those poker players. We all know them. They're the ones who hold their proverbial cards close to the vest. When we withhold information or feed it to the project stakeholders on a "need to know" basis, we are not being transparent, and others might well question our agenda. Have you ever known people who were master poker players in all their communications? The ones who feed you one item at a time? When we hold onto information because we know that information is power, rather than sharing information because we know that sharing information not only is power but also a key to getting projects done quickly, we are sure to win a trust-busting award.

5. **Share confidential information.** Sometimes, however, there really is a need to withhold information. When we have accepted the responsibility of hearing or reading confidential information, we cannot share it and leave our integrity intact. Some people have a need to "be in the loop." Such people ask, "Can you keep a secret?" or "If I tell you something, do you promise not to repeat it?" or "I really shouldn't mention this but...." We need to be careful before listening to the confidential information. We want to avoid the conundrum of whether to share vital information if it means breaking our promise and therefore being out of integrity. If we're comfortable with this dilemma, share and listen to confidential information, and you will certainly bust trust.

---

10 Ways to Bust Trust

1. Gossip.
2. Use humor inappropriately.
3. Be competitive.
4. Withhold information.
5. Share confidential information.
6. Don't make/meet commitments.
7. Don't prepare.
8. Act inconsistently.
9. Be ethnocentric.
10. Believe that results rule.

6. **Don't make or meet commitments.** Remember that boss who never had to meet his commitments because he never would make any? Making commitments means taking a stand. However, making commitments without meeting them is a great way to lose credibility. When we stall, put off work, or simply don't get the job done, others lose confidence in us. And we open ourselves up to micromanagement. People who are dependent on our results and have made commitments to others understandably get really nervous when the results are delayed. They're on the hook because of their own commitments. And when nervous, they tend to hover. One of our best defenses against micromanagement is to meet our commitments—and communicate if we can't.

7. **Don't prepare.** When we don't do our homework, we lose credibility. When we're asked a question and have to admit that we don't have an answer and are forced to say, "I'll get back to you on that one," we lose credibility. Sure, saying that you'll get an answer is better than making up an answer, but it's no substitute for being prepared. So if we don't anticipate questions, we're likely to be asked, and if we don't prepare answers in advance, we will lose credibility, which is a great way to bust trust.

8. **Act inconsistently.** Acting consistently is a cornerstone of building trust, so when we don't, we can be pretty certain that people won't trust us. Consistency is having values and matching our behavior to our values. It's about "walking the talk." It's about behavior that people can count on. It's about reliability. So when we react inconsistently, such as when we react emotionally to unexpected bad news and shoot the proverbial messenger in the process, we will be effective at busting trust.

9. **Be closed to other cultures/ethnocentric.** In a nutshell, ethnocentrism is the belief that my culture is better than yours. The culture in question might be organizational culture, national culture, regional culture, age, gender, religion, or a host of other cultures. When we close ourselves off to input from people who are different from us, we let them know that neither they nor their ideas are important. Not only will we bust their trust, but we will lose credibility with other team members as well.

10. **Believe that results rule.** When we put results ahead of relationships, we pretty much guarantee that we'll get those results at the expense of trust and without the collaboration and cooperation that we'll need for long-lasting success. Getting results is fine. But getting them at the expense of others means they'll be short-term results at best. Failure to collaborate is a great way to bust trust.

> **TIP**
>
> Getting results is fine. But getting them at the expense of others means they'll be short-term results at best. Failure to collaborate is a great way to bust trust.

Restoring Trust and Healing

We all betray trust at one point or another. The betrayal might be very small, causing few consequences, large with major impacts, or any place in between. Dennis Reina and Michelle Reina address the subject of trust and betrayal in their Reina Trust and Behavior model.[23]

According to this model, we all experience betrayal of trust in "personal and work relationships occurring on a continuum from minor to major, from intentional to unintentional."[24] They have created the Seven Steps for Healing, which include:

1. *Observe and acknowledge what has happened.* When we're in the middle of restoring trust, it's often hard to be objective. However, in order to heal, we need this acknowledgment.

2. *Allow feelings to surface.* The feelings in question include both those of the betrayer as well as those of the betrayed. Although difficult, we need to create a space for ourselves and others where feelings can surface.

3. *Get and provide support.* Again, Reina and Reina's model is geared towards leaders helping employees through organizational transitions, such as mergers and acquisitions. However, this advice to get help applies for project teams as well. The project manager might solicit help from other project managers, from their bosses, from human resources, from friends, colleagues, at home, etc.

4. *Reframe the experience,* which involves giving it context. Ask questions of the other party(ies) to clarify the experience from their perspective.

5. *Take responsibility,* which can only happen when we acknowledge our mistakes and shed our defensiveness. Taking responsibility also involves making commitments, keeping future promises, and managing expectations.

6. *Forgive yourself and others.* Holding on to emotions, such as defensiveness, anger, and resentment takes energy, which is better spent on healing.

7. *Let go and move on.* Letting go does not mean that we dismiss what has happened. It means that we accept it and our part in it. It means that we are committed to a more trusting future.

Although Reina and Reina look at trust and betrayal from the perspective of organizational leaders and what can occur with mergers and acquisitions, this model is useful and can be applied generally.

Remember that while we can attempt to restore trust, we can't force others to trust us. We can take responsibility for our part in the breakdown. We can try to open communications with the other parties. But we cannot demand that others restore their trust in us.

Although this model portrays the seven steps in linear fashion, individuals may experience many steps at a time or may backtrack and "re-experience" a previous step.

Requirements and Trust

If the people from whom we are eliciting requirements do not trust us, they will find many reasons to procrastinate. They will find many ways to try to prevent the project from moving forward. If you've ever heard any or all of the following, and you can fill in the blanks with the words "new or changed requirements," there is a strong possibility that the business expert is trying to find a way to hinder the progress of the project.

> *"Did I tell you that? That's plain wrong. What I really need is [new requirements]."*

> *"I'm so sorry, but I forgot to tell you [new requirements]."*

> *"I'm sure I mentioned that [new requirements]."*

> *"Oh by the way, [new requirements]."*

Or you might have heard statements from key stakeholders like the following, which will probably result in decisions being revisited.

"I don't have time to meet. I'm up to my eyeballs."

"I can't attend that meeting, but I'll send Susan. She is empowered to make decisions." Somehow, however, Susan really does not have the authority to make business decisions. Either she says she needs to discuss those decisions with the key stakeholders or those key stakeholders override her decisions.

"Sorry I'm late. Just continue on without me. I'll catch up later."

Sometimes these excuses are given aggressively and sometimes more passive-aggressively but always with the same message: "Things are working just fine the way they are. Please go away and let us do our jobs!" On the surface, this type of comment sounds reasonable. However, when we dig beneath the surface, this procrastination or, worse, outright sabotage means that the stakeholder does not want the change to be implemented.

Distrust and the Fear Factor

The most common reason for stakeholder caution and concern is distrust, caused by fear, which we will discuss further in Chapter 8, Developing the Courage To Be Influential.

Usually the fear relates to one or more of the following:

> **TIP**
>
> 1. Assess commitment individually.
> 2. Address individual concerns.
> 3. Address negative behavior.
> 4. Recognize individual and group achievement.

- Fear that the end product,
  such as a new system, will dramatically change or eliminate their jobs.

- Fear that the end product will impede or slow their workflow in the name of trying to improve it.
- Fear that familiar tools and software (existing system or Excel spreadsheets) will be incomplete, inaccurate, or difficult to learn.
- Fear that they will no longer be experts (remember that expert power?).

These fears, real or imagined, can cause stakeholders to do whatever they can to postpone the inevitable implementation of the new product or service. Without an established relationship and trust, it will be very difficult for analysts and project managers to elicit the necessary requirements.

Elicitation Techniques for Building Trust

There are a variety of techniques that are typically used in requirements elicitation. One of the most common is the requirements workshop, a facilitated session in which a facilitator enables key stakeholders to articulate their requirements in a formal meeting. This approach has many advantages, including using the synergy of the group to build relationships and trust.

Another common technique is the one-on-one interview. This technique is a way for business analysts and project managers to meet individually with stakeholders. Through these individual meetings, trust can be built in several ways:

- *Assess commitment.* Some stakeholders do not like to make decisions or agree to decisions in meetings. One-on-one meetings provide a safer venue to discuss real needs behind the stated—and unstated—needs.

- *Address individual concerns.* Some individuals are more inclined to reveal their true concerns about the project and the other project stakeholders in one-on-one interviews, rather than in large groups. When elicitation is limited to facilitated sessions, these concerns go largely unaddressed.

- *Address negative behavior.* Sometimes stakeholders either dominate meetings or demonstrate various types of behavior that negatively impact the group. By meeting individually, analysts and project managers can focus on the behavior, and together with the individual, determine ways to reduce its impact.

- *Recognize individual achievement.* There are individuals who are not comfortable with public recognition. Individual accomplishments are better recognized in private with such stakeholders.

Each of these individual meetings is a chance to establish rapport and ultimately build relationships and trust.

 # *Summary*

Let's recap what we've covered in this chapter:

- Defined and understood the meaning of trust
- Looked at practical project applications of some of the concepts in Stephen M.R. Covey's book, The Speed of Trust, and provided many ways to build and destroy trust, as well as a process for healing when trust has been destroyed.
- Provided tips for building trust when eliciting requirements and clues for determining when the trust is not there.

---

1   Kieron Ohara and Will Hutton. Trust: From Socrates to Spin. (Cambridge: Icon Books, 2004).

2   Tom Peters, "Speed is Life: Go Fast or Go Broke," Enterprise Media, accessed July 25, 2012, http://www.enterprisemedia.com/product/00014/speed_life_fast_broke.html.

3   Stephen M.R. Covey. The SPEED of Trust: The One Thing That Changes Everything (New York: Free Press, 2008).

4   David H. Maister, et al. The Trusted Advisor. (New York: Simon & Schuster, 2000).

5   Charles H. Green, Trusted Advisor Associates, accessed June 27, 2012, http://trustedadvisor.com/.

6   Dennis S. Reina and Michelle L. Reina, "Building Sustainable Trust," OD Practitioner Vol 39 No 1 2007, Accessed June 26, 2012, http://www.systemsinsync.com/pdfs/Building%20Sustainable%20Trust.pdf.

7   Tom Crann, "Bridge survivor on 5th anniversary: 'The day I got to live,'" Minnesota Public Radio, accessed July 31, 2012, http://minnesota.publicradio.org/display/web/2012/07/31/disaster/qa-bridge-collapse-anniversary/.

8   Dr. Robert F. Hurley, Professor of Management, NY, The Decision to Trust, 2006.

9   Ibid.

10 Dictionary.com, accessed January 19, 2012, http://dictionary.reference.com/browse/trust.

11 Christian Andrew, "General Motors Beats Toyota and Regaining No. 1 Spot", April 24, 2011, Accessed January 22, 2012,http://www.dbwnews.com/280/general-motors-beats-toyota-and-regaining-no-1-spot.html dbwnews.com.

12 "Quotations: Character," Josephson Institute, accessed March 02, 2012, http://josephsoninstitute.org/quotes/quotations.php?q=Character.

13 Dictionary.com, accessed February 24, 2012, http://dictionary.reference.com/browse/tragic+flaw.

14 For an interesting twist on this story, one in which Iago is honest and sympathetic, read I, Iago, by Nicole Galland, (2012).

15 "The Six Pillars of Character®", Josephson Institute, accessed March 02, 2012, http://charactercounts.org/sixpillars.html .

16 IIBA and Kevin Brennan. A Guide to the Business Analysis Body of Knowledge® (BABOK® Guide), 2nd ed. West Valley City, UT: Waking Lion Press, 2009. Section 8.2.3.

17 John Richardson. "Topics For Discussion: What Is Integrity?", Success Begins Today, accessed March 02, 2012, http://successbeginstoday.org/wordpress/2007/09/topics-for-discussion-what-is-integrity/.

18 Stephen M.R. Covey. The SPEED of Trust: The One Thing That Changes Everything (New York: Free Press, 2008). 87.

19 Android, accessed March 02, 2012, http://developer.android.com/reference/android/content/Intent.html.

20 Glenn Paskin, "Seven Secrets of a Joyful Life," excerpt from Family Circle Magazine, Dr. Wayne W. Dyer's enewsletter, accessed March 02, 2012, http://www.drwaynedyer.com/articles/seven-secrets-of-a-joyful-life.

21 "Quotes About Honesty", Goodreads, accessed March 02, 2012, http://www.goodreads.com/quotes/tag/honesty.

22 Sophocles (496-406 BC), Quote cited from Brainy Quote, accessed March 02, 2012, http://www.brainyquote.com/quotes/quotes/s/sophocles388468.html.

23 Dennis S. Reina and Michelle L. Reina, "Building Sustainable Trust," OD Practitioner Vol 39 No 1 2007, accessed June 26, 2012, http://www.systemsinsync.com/pdfs/Building%20Sustainable%20Trust.pdf.

24 Ibid.

04 Influential Preparation

"*Before anything else, preparation is the key to success.*"

ALEXANDER GRAHAM BELL

As a trusted advisor, we need to be well-prepared. There are many aspects to the preparation work that we need to do.

Background

We all know preparation is important, yet we often just wing it. Whether it's due to the inevitable time crunches, lack of support, or a perceived absence of need, we frequently don't do an adequate job. We might think we can influence others by force of will or personality, but that won't be a very repeatable process.

Have you consistently been influential without adequate preparation? We haven't!

Influencing Techniques

There are a myriad techniques that can be used for the preparation phase of influencing others. Some techniques that might be mistaken for influence are actually persuading or convincing types of techniques. We will concentrate on the techniques most helpful with the preparation aspect of influence. Two of them, stakeholder analysis and consulting skills, are so important we will cover them later in their own chapters. The techniques most helpful in preparing for influence are:

- Networking.
- Building Coalitions.
- The Huddle.
- Planting Seeds.
- Stakeholder Analysis (separate chapter).
- Consultation/Advising (separate chapters).

Networking

Networking is a way to make connections with others to both provide and receive something. In business, it is often associated with industry groups of some sort, such as professional organizations, job-seeking groups, or markets for sales lead generation. Networking within an organization takes much the same form. Your company may have special interest groups, such as a "Project Management Forum" or a "Business Analysis Community of Practice." These are networking opportunities that can lead to valuable connections.

NETWORKING

Networking is a way to prepare to influence others through the relationships and contacts that are made in your network.

Effective networking can help make contacts, which leads to connections, and ultimately, for receiving value. Networking is a way to prepare to influence others through the relationships and contacts that are made in your network.

The concept of networking is a whole subject and can occupy volumes of books and articles. One source describes networking this way: "Networking isn't a process of making cold-calls or sending Friend or "Join my Network" requests to people you don't know. It's connecting to people you *do* know through a valid connection."[1]

Before going further, let us make it clear that we do not view networking as the stereotypical mingling among extroverted types. A practical guide to networking defines it as "...the art of building and maintaining connections for shared positive outcomes."[2] The author's take is that networking for deep and lasting connections is best performed by introverts and "centroverts" as she puts is (a centrovert being in the middle between introvert and extrovert).

We leave the nuances and details of networking to more focused sources. What we have found is that networking is a great way to build trust as well as coalitions. We'll cover the latter in a moment. By spending time networking, we form and build *connections*; we don't just make contacts or get information or leads. True, the people you network with can help you, and that is one reason to network. But, to do it effectively, your goal is the long-term connection and the exchange of giving and receiving, not just the immediate completion of a task or getting a sale.

We've noticed that auto salespeople, realtors, and even clothing salespeople have vastly improved their connecting and networking skills. They realize that you may not be currently in the market for what they sell, but you might be in the future. We get birthday cards every year from our car salesperson, even though we buy a car only every few years. The realtor who sold us a house sends calendars every year to stay connected even though we bought our house several years ago. She wants us to remember her, of course. She also hopes that we will pass her name on to others even if we don't want to buy or sell a house right now.

If you are seeking influence using the "position-related currency," you can gain visibility by networking. This benefit of networking can be especially helpful—and necessary—in larger organizations. In any size organization, it is helpful to work on your networking skills.

Social Networking

A rapidly growing trend that is likely to continue is the ability to network with a broader population through social media or social networking services. For business, the most popular networks are LinkedIn, Twitter, and Google+. Facebook has made inroads into business, but we think it has mostly a social and not primarily a business focus. The same considerations for using electronic networking apply as they do to in-person networking.

As noted in an earlier chapter, a dramatic example of influence through social networking was the so-called "Arab Spring" of 2011. Social media was credited with spreading the message of revolution in Egypt, Libya, and Tunisia, where it probably would not have been possible verbally or in-person. It also helped to bring the participants into a coalition, a subject we'll cover shortly.

It is also easy to confuse "following" or "linking in" with someone or being in their "circle" with actual networking. Social networking providers make it very easy to request someone join your network and to accept such requests. The authors both make and receive such requests as often as anyone. We are still learning as most people are to make the electronic network succeed as more than a collection of connections. Our advice:

- Be generous when people request to join your network.
- If you want to separate out categories of contacts, join and use Google+.
- Participate in discussion forums; LinkedIn has every conceivable special-interest group on which you can ask and answer questions. It's an excellent way to become familiar with issues relevant to your domain.
- If you feel a need to influence the broader community you work in, use Twitter and tweet regularly.

- Don't post about how cute your kids are or that your cat just threw up on your laptop. Use Facebook for that kind of post if you can't resist.
- Post your thoughts or lessons learned or good articles or links to good books. Ask probing questions. Share your experiences.
- Don't lecture. (Whoops, that sounds like a lecture—a book or class is the place for that, not on social media!)

Considerations

Networking, whether in-person or through social media, takes time and won't immediately pay off. In an article titled "10 Tips for Successful Business Networking," the website, businessknowhow.com, says, "Keep in mind that networking is about being genuine and authentic, building trust and relationships, and seeing how you can help others."[3] These are important aspects of the Influencing Formula and usually take time to pay dividends.

Networking isn't always effective. We may end up making connections with people who can't or won't help us. Or we connect with people who we can't help or who only want our help. In building our training business, we know this all too well. We regularly attend and speak at project management and business analysis conferences around the world. We've met some of the most interesting, friendliest, expert professionals you can imagine. While such relationships are often personally satisfying (or frustrating, in a few cases), they may not accomplish our goal of influencing others.

It's not easy discerning which contacts are good to network with and which are not. It also takes time to build relationships from those contacts, and sometimes they end up being satisfying friendships and will not help you to achieve influence.

Our Advice:

- Do a mini "lessons learned" from each networking opportunity like you might do for a project.
- Spend time thinking about the contacts you make, and categorize them into Influential, Relationship-Only, or Avoid. Then follow up accordingly.
- Seek out and ask for help from expert networkers you know. Observe how others network through social media and adopt the practices and styles you admire.
- Keep a list of names of who to contact for different parts of your projects.
- Know what you need and who to go to when you need help.

Building Coalitions

A coalition temporarily pulls together individuals or groups who otherwise might not be logically or formally joined to accomplish some goal or achieve an objective. Coalitions might exist to oppose nuclear waste, to get funding for a new sports stadium, or to form a voting bloc in a legislative body.

A formal definition for a coalition is "a temporary alliance or partnering of groups in order to achieve a common purpose or to engage in joint activity.[4]"

In business, a coalition might be a group of disparate stakeholders who have a vested interest in solving a business problem or accomplishing a project outcome.

> **COALITIONS**
>
> Coalitions pull together individuals or groups who otherwise might not be formally joined to accomplish some goal or achieve an objective.

They may be naturally formed by a group of stakeholders on a project. Quite often, coalitions are formed by people who are not initially connected but have some common interest. For example, take the problem of customer complaints about product quality at a computer manufacturer. A business or process analyst might discover the root causes of the quality problems are shared between the production department and the parts procurement division. Those two entities could be formed into a coalition to solve the problem.

Considerations

Coalitions have several advantages for exerting influence.

- First, they provide backing and support for the person or group trying to influence something. By leveraging others, it may be possible to achieve more than one person or a smaller group could do on their own. Again, the "Arab Spring" serves as a dramatic reminder of this.

- A coalition also brings strength in numbers, which may be necessary when facing a hostile opposition. One organization in which we train has ongoing issues between union and management over working conditions and safety conditions. The union provides workers with this safety in numbers that would not exist otherwise.

- Groups can also provide better solutions than individuals can generate. They can leverage the "wisdom of crowds," as financial journalist James Surowiecki describes in his 2005 book, *The Wisdom of Crowds*. He maintains that a diverse group of concerned stakeholders is always smarter than the smartest people in the group.[5] This is another way of stating an advantage of coalitions and how they might prove influential.

There are several possible side-effects or drawbacks of coalitions though.

- First, special-interest groups can be divisive. One only has to look at political or religious groups, or even rival sports teams, to see many examples of divisiveness in action. In organizations, when groups or coalitions form, it can lead to gossiping or taking sides, and this outcome usually breaks trust that people in those groups may have built with others in the organization. The reason? People outside the coalition may not understand and may distrust the reason the coalition was formed, rejecting its aims. This very result is the opposite of what the group intends because distrust typically precludes the ability to influence.

- Because coalitions are often informal, they can lack the structure that more formal organizations have. Hidden agendas can develop in those situations, which can similarly break down trust.

- If people with similar interests are dispersed, it is harder to form a coalition. Just as meetings in general are more difficult to facilitate virtually, coalition-building is more challenging electronically. That may in part be due to the difficulty of forging the emotional bonds that coalitions need in order to be effective. It is hard to imagine the "Occupy Wall Street" coalitions in the fall of 2011 having much impact if they tried to conduct their "occupations" via computer. One could argue whether or not the protesters were influential, but they certainly garnered media interest, so they accomplished at least one goal.

- Because coalitions are groups, they have the same challenges as other groups or teams in the workplace. To be effective, they need to go through the same stages of development as any other team. After forming, they can suffer from "storming," and the resulting conflict can break the coalition. If the group cannot overcome the potential competition for roles and responsibilities, especially related to leadership and decision-making, it can never move to the "norming" stage. Without that, the group can never truly "perform," Tuckman's fourth stage of team dynamics.[6]

- Balancing the concepts of influence and pressure is difficult but necessary. Large groups may fall prey to the temptation to pressure others into doing what they want rather than influencing them. The larger the group, the easier it is to resort to pressure without the necessary trust and preparation needed to be influential. For example, political candidates often feel "pressured" to abandon their candidacy when enough people in their party call for them to withdraw.

Our Advice:

- Know the power and motivation each person brings to the coalition.
- Work with participants and convince them to help sell the coalition's ideas to executives and sponsors.
- Understand the coalition's agendas and guide the group to work towards a common goal that is aligned with the organization's values and goals.

HUDDLES

Informal gatherings, either spontaneously or planned, with people you want to influence.

The Huddle

A huddle is any informal gathering to meet with people you want to influence.

It gets its name from sports, such as American or Canadian football, soccer, cricket, and basketball. In football, the offensive team huddles before a play. The football type of huddle is used for one-way communication for the quarterback to convey the next play to the rest of the offense. There is minimal interaction and concise communication because of time pressures.

A business huddle can be used for many things, including updating others on status, sharing information, or voicing concerns or questions. It may be a regular daily event, such as a morning stand-up meeting. Or it might be periodic, unscheduled sessions for updates or brainstorming.

Huddles increase interaction, help to develop relationships, increase morale, and foster trust among the people involved.

Considerations

Huddles have these advantages for influencing others.

- Because of their ability to foster relationships and sharing, huddles can help build trust, a key component for influencing.
- Huddles can promote communication, increase the quality of it, and decrease the time spent. Numerous, lengthy, spread-out emails on a topic can instead be quickly dealt with in a huddle.
- Face-to-face huddles in particular can increase the effect or emotional value attached to what is being communicated and improve outcomes. Remember that only 7% of the meaning of communication comes from the words we use, while 38% comes from the tone of voice, and 55% from other non-verbal communication, such as facial expressions and body language. [7]

There are some disadvantages of huddles:

- If not managed, huddles can turn into gossip sessions or, at best, a friendly break from other tasks. Ground rules can help prevent this negative outcome.
- Huddles may evolve into gripe sessions if the team is not careful. Often the reason to huddle is to solve problems. When discussing problems, it is very easy to digress and complain about our favorite subjects, and again, ground rules may be needed to prevent this.
- Because they may appear to be time-wasting chit-chat sessions, some organizations may view huddles as not being productive. Huddles foster relationships and may improve morale, so people may actually appear happy or even laugh during them. That's actually a good sign, as long as the huddle is a means to an end and not an end in itself. Keeping huddles short may be enough to overcome this perception.

Our Advice:

- Use huddles with colocated groups that either will help you contribute to influencing others or contain stakeholders you wish to influence.
- Keep huddle sessions short. Make sure everyone knows the objective and desired outcome, like any meeting. Use simple ground rules to keep the huddle from veering off into gossip or gripe sessions.
- Come prepared to the group with your goals and ideas, and know what you want to discuss.
- Know what each person's strength is, and listen to each person's ideas.

Planting Seeds

This form of preparation for influence is the closest to marketing and persuasion of all the types of preparation we cover. It is the concept of starting with an idea, expanding on it, adding to the evidence over time, and slowly convincing people of a position.

> **PLANTING SEEDS**
>
> Starts with a concept and adds more ideas and evidence over time to build toward receptivity for a recommendation.

Examples of where this type of preparation might be useful include establishing a PMO (Project Management Office) or a BA-COE (Business Analysis Center of Excellence). It is also effective when trying to get management adoption of Business Process Management. These types of initiatives typically involve a shift in organizational culture and require time to adopt. The planting and then nurturing of seeds over time can help the organization understand the purpose and benefits of a PMO or a COE and become more comfortable with the change required.

Planting seeds is similar to the marketing approach called "drip marketing" or a "drip campaign" in which the seed is planted, and then the influencer provides periodic messages and communication related to the seed. The name comes from drip irrigation, a technique for watering seeds and plants over time. "Drip marketing is popularly applied as a sales tool, particularly in long sales-cycles (large ticket items or enterprise-level sales). Whereas persistent follow-up can become a deterrent to closing the sale, Drip Marketing methods offer the ability to remain top-of-mind, and even prompt action, without jeopardizing the relationship."[8]

The idea is to analyze your stakeholders enough to determine if you have a prospect with the potential of buying your idea. For example, a prospect may be executives with the budget to establish a PMO. Then, by providing relevant information spread over time about the recommendation, a drip campaign would keep the idea of a PMO fresh in the decision-makers' minds. Examples of relevant information might include articles about how PMOs benefit other organizations, things learned at conferences about them, internal presentations on the subject, etc. The key is to avoid irritating the decision makers by asking for approval too soon or often. Instead, the ideal outcome would be to present a business case after the seeds have been planted and nourished and then obtain a favorable decision to proceed.

Considerations

Planting seeds can assist your influence in the following ways:

- This technique allows persistence without being obnoxious. By building your case over time and adding to your prep work repeatedly, you can keep your idea "top-of-mind" without being annoying.
- Less preparation is needed for each "watering" of your idea, but the overall process is of longer duration.
- Planting time is quick, and you can get started immediately. For example, you can circulate an article on a BA-COE right now.

There are some possible disadvantages to planting seeds:

- Long duration takes patience and persistence. If you need quick action, this technique is not appropriate.
- Follow-up is required. The key to planting seeds or drip marketing is to apply regular, periodic "watering" of your seed. The approach weakens, and the seed will wither and die if you stop your follow-up.
- The original seed needs more information added over time to be influential. This is not so much a negative as it is a reminder to be patient, keep providing new information, and don't rehash what you may have already provided.

Our Advice:

Determine if the thing you want to influence is appropriate for a seed-planting approach. Our examples of a COE or management adoption of a BPM approach are typical things that take time to accomplish and would be appropriate.

- Be patient and prepared for months, or even years in some cases, to accomplish your goal.
- Keep track of all the "drips" you have applied, and add them to an eventual business case. Make the business case the culmination of all your prep work.
- For simpler "seed planting," use this approach to let people know something will happen in the future, such as a change in methodology or a department re-organization. In sports terms, this is also known as a heads-up.

Summary

Preparation is one of the main ingredients in the influencing formula. For those of us who rely on expert power to influence, our preparation skills become key to helping us improve our ability to influence.

Table 5 lists a summary of the six techniques, including the two covered in separate chapters, and how they can help prepare for influencing. The techniques we covered in this chapter include:

- Networking
- Building Coalitions
- The Huddle
- Planting Seeds

Summary of Preparation Techniques	
Technique	**Purpose**
Networking	This is a way to prepare to influence others through relationships and contacts that are made in your network.
Building Coalitions	Coalitions pull together individuals or groups who otherwise might not be formally joined to accomplish some goal or achieve an objective.
The Huddle	Informal gatherings, either spontaneous or planned, with people you want to influence.
Planting Seeds	Starts with a concept, and adds more ideas and evidence over time to build toward receptivity for a recommendation.
Stakeholder Analysis	Understanding the roles, authority levels, influence, and acceptance of stakeholders.
Consultation/ Advising	Using consulting skills and consultative questioning to understand business problems and make recommendations as a way of influencing.

TABLE 5: Preparation Techniques Summary

Considerations

- Do a mini "lessons learned" from each networking opportunity like you might do for a project.
- Spend time thinking about the contacts you make, and categorize them into Influential, Relationship-Only, or Avoid. Then, follow up accordingly.
- Seek out and ask for help from experts.
- Keep a list of names of who to contact for different parts of your projects.
- Know what you need and who to go to when you need help.

- They provide backing and support for the person or group trying to influence something.
- This brings strength in numbers, which may be necessary when facing a "hostile" opposition.
- Groups can often provide better solutions than individuals.

- Most effective with colocated groups that either will help you contribute to influencing others or contain stakeholders you wish to influence.
- Increases interaction, helps to develop relationships, increases morale, and fosters trust among the people involved.
- Keep sessions short. Come prepared, and understand the group.

- Analyze your stakeholders enough to determine if you have a prospect with the potential of buying your idea.
- Allows persistence without being obnoxious.
- Less preparation needed for each "watering" of your idea.
- Planting time is quick, and you can get started immediately.

- Builds trust and helps gain insights into stakeholder preferences and motivations.
- Helps to understand possible resistance to our recommendations and to leverage champions to our cause.
- See Chapter 5 for details.

- Consultation is the best way, in our opinion, of exerting expert power to assert our influence.
- A consulting approach helps us to be courageous.
- See Chapters 6 and 7 for details.

1   "What is a Network?" The Riley Guide, accessed August 22, 2012, http://www.
    rileyguide.com/network.html.

2   Devora Zack. *Networking for People Who Hate Networking: A Field Guide for Introverts,
    the Overwhelmed, and the Underconnected.* (San Francisco, CA: Berrett-Koehler
    Publishers, 2010), 4.

3   Stephanie Speisman, "10 Tips for Successful Business Networking," Business Know-
    How, accessed July 23, 2012, http://www.businessknowhow.com/tips/networking.htm.

4. Douglas H. Yarn, *The Dictionary of Conflict Resolution.* (San Francisco: Jossey-Bass
    Publishers, 1991), 81.

5   James Surowiecki. *The Wisdom of Crowds.* (New York, NY: Anchor Books, 2005).

6   "Tuckman forming storming norming performing model." *Businessballs,*
    accessed December 09, 2011, http://www.businessballs.com/
    tuckmanformingstormingnormingperforming.htm.

7   Albert Mehrabian and Morton Wiener. *Journal of Personality and Social Psychology,* Vol
    6(1), May 1967, 109-114, accessed June 11, 2012, http://psycnet.apa.org/journals/
    psp/6/1/109/.

8   Drip marketing. *Wikipedia, the free encyclopedia,* accessed December 10, 2011, http://
    en.wikipedia.org/wiki/Drip_marketing.

05 Stakeholder Analysis

"When dealing with people, remember you are not dealing with creatures of logic, but creatures of emotion."

DALE CARNEGIE

In the earlier chapter on preparation, we covered influence preparation techniques, such as Networking, Building Coalitions, the Huddle, and Planting Seeds. Another essential preparation technique is to understand and analyze the stakeholders we are trying to influence.

Background

The task/technique of stakeholder analysis is an integral one in business analysis and project management because of the importance of stakeholders to success in these fields. Stakeholder analysis may be even more important as we work towards the role of trusted advisor.

It is much easier to influence others if we understand their outlook, work style, and personality. To quote Stephen Covey, "Seek first to understand, then to be understood."[1] Covey could easily have been talking about influence here. By analyzing stakeholders, we seek to understand the:

- Personality type and preferences of our stakeholders.
- Degree of acceptance and influence of stakeholders.
- Factors that decision-makers will use for making their decisions.

Simply working with stakeholders may give you clues and ideas of their preferences and how best to communicate with them. Those clues may provide insights into the decision-making style of the person you are trying to influence. We know what you might be thinking.

How do you best make use of those clues? What clues are most helpful to watch for? First let's explore stakeholders in general.

What Is a Stakeholder?

Stakeholders have a stake or vested interest in the project or its result, whether individually or as a group. They will be impacted either positively or negatively (or both) by the project, the business analysis work, and the end-product. Technically speaking, if people or groups are not affected by a project or its resulting product, they are not strictly stakeholders.

Stakeholders may be but do not have to be decision-makers. They may represent the interests of another group of stakeholders.[2] For example, a business-representative (e.g., subject matter expert) may represent him or herself and also a group of stakeholders, such as a division or branch, an organization, or government agency.

There is a two-way relationship between stakeholders and projects. We need to pay attention to stakeholders because they influence each other. Many stakeholders strongly influence the project phase(s) and vice versa; the project and product deliverables will strongly influence how the stakeholders will react during all project activities.

Key stakeholder responsibilities include:

- Taking ownership of the information and defining the requirements affecting them.
- Producing, reviewing, and/or approving key deliverables.
- Making timely decisions applicable to their domain.
- Reviewing/approving their requirements.
- Being available for meetings.
- Resolving issues in a timely manner.

Stakeholders can sabotage projects with resistance to change and by not taking responsibility for the areas mentioned above. (Not all stakeholders are difficult, of course, but if only a few were difficult, then we would hardly need a topic on analyzing them!) See Chapter 9, Influencing Difficult Stakeholders, for more information on this topic.

Stakeholders, though, can be as varied as the many types of people who work in an organization. To help influence them, a small amount of analysis can go a long way. Let us explore five steps for analyzing stakeholders and planning an approach that will help engage and influence them to cooperate toward achieving the common goals of the organization and/or a project.

Key Stakeholder Analysis Tasks

There are five essential tasks when analyzing stakeholders, summarized in *Figure 3* . We show the tasks as cyclical because analyzing and interacting with stakeholders is an ongoing process.

Stakeholder Analysis

1. Identify Required Roles

2. Define Authorization Levels

3. Categorize Stakeholders

4. Analyze Stakeholder Influence

5. Plan for Maximizing Influence

FIGURE 3: Stakeholder Analysis Tasks

We will present the tasks in the following order, knowing that they could be and often are performed iteratively.

1. **Identify the Required Roles.**
2. **Define Authorization Levels.**
3. **Categorize Stakeholders.**
4. **Analyze Stakeholder Influence.**
5. **Plan Approach to Maximize Influence.**

1. Identify the Required Roles

The first stakeholder process we need to perform is identifying which roles will be required for a project or phase of a project, such as business analysis, design, or testing. Depending on the end-product, approach, methodology, and location of stakeholders, different roles may be needed. For example, we will need different roles for building a bridge than for enhancing software. Building a bridge may require software, to be sure, but it will almost certainly have additional required roles for environmental impact analysis, community relations, and working with other city, state, and federal agencies.

Projects using different approaches and methodologies, such as Waterfall or Agile, SCRUM, Rational Unified Process, Microsoft Solutions Framework, or Prince 2 all have different designated roles that must be filled. If some of the project work is distributed to different countries, additional legal, facilitator, or contact person roles might be required. A business analyst or project manager needs to identify and document all the roles that will be needed in the various phases (e.g., business case, initiating, planning, executing, managing, and closing). When considering project roles, remember that roles are what people do on the project and not a specific "job title."

Project professionals also need to get stakeholder agreement on who is responsible for specific work. Many organizations have standard roles and responsibilities for each project.

Some common key stakeholder roles include:

- Sponsor: The sponsor not only obtains the project funding but is the key "mover and shaker" or champion of a project. Sponsors approve the scope of the project, the final requirements, and major changes to the scope and requirements baseline and accept the final product.

- Project Manager (PM): Ultimately responsible for meeting the project objectives[3], PMs oversee project tasks, including planning, executing, and closing all project work. A major responsibility is for coordinating communication with stakeholders across the project. During project execution and control, the project manager tracks progress against the plans and takes actions as necessary to ensure that the project performance is satisfactory. The PM is also responsible for keeping the sponsor informed of the project status and working closely with the project sponsor on issues of major importance to the project.

- *Business Analyst*: According to the *BABOK® Guide 2.0*, business analysis is "a set of tasks and techniques used to work as a liaison among stakeholders in order to understand the structure, policies, and operations of an organization, and recommend solutions that enable the organization to achieve its goals."[4] The business analyst role is to complete those tasks, including the work needed to elicit, analyze, and validate requirements. Business analysts also make solution recommendations based on analysis of business and technical impacts.

- *Business Domain Subject Matter Expert (SME):* Often known as clients, customers, product owners, or business experts, SMEs represent sponsors, who are ultimately accountable for getting the end-product they want and, therefore, defining their requirements. Sponsors usually delegate the detailed definition to business stakeholders who will be impacted by the end-product. They are usually heavily involved in elicitation meetings. SMEs provide their expertise about the current situation ("as-is") and about the future state ("to-be") relating to the new product and associated business processes resulting from the change. Business SMEs may be end-users (who use the end-product directly), supervisors, managers, business process owners, or others who ideally have been assigned by the sponsor to provide their input. A few examples of SMEs are:
  - A retail store buyer defining requirements of a system to offer substitutions automatically when the ordered item is not in stock.
  - A financial analyst in a software company.
  - An external consultant brought in to provide expertise in a specific business area, such as offering a new product or service.
  - Staff who work in city, state, or federal agencies, such as a representative from the Bureau of Criminal Apprehension brought in to define requirements of a new crime prevention system.
  - A logistics manager on a project to automate a distribution center.
  - A doctor on a project to automate medical records.
- *Technical Domain Subject Matter Expert (SME):* There are often many specialists on project teams. System and

process designers, database analysts, networking specialists, product developers, product testers, and call center staff are all examples of key technical stakeholders needed to create, update, and support IT end-products. Other industries will have their own specialists, including architects, engineers, financial analysts, marketing specialists, environmental technicians, etc. Whatever the specialty, the technical domain SMEs need to understand the requirements from their perspective while ensuring the feasibility of the requirements from a technical perspective.

- *Regulators:* Representatives from the legal, compliance, audit, or regulation enforcement areas are also stakeholders. These stakeholders may be internal to the performing organization or from an external regulatory agency.

- *Vendors:* Vendors who are external to the organization and who provide goods or services to the organization can also be stakeholders. For example, if the project solution is the purchase of commercial software, the vendors supplying that software need to understand the business requirements of the performing organization in order to ensure that the software meets those requirements.

- *Solution Implementers:* On projects where the end-product requires extensive changes within the organization, division, or business unit, there may be staff assigned to help with the implementation (see *BABOK® Guide 2.0 Knowledge Area Solution Assessment and Validation*).

2. Define Authorization Levels

In order to influence stakeholders, we need to know who the decision-makers are. Clarifying authorization levels for approvals helps steer us to project influencers and decision-makers.

During projects, all the responsibilities and authorization levels for each major role need to be defined (again, what people do rather than a specific "job title"). Authorization levels describe who approves different aspects of the project work. The business analyst or project manager often facilitates the conversation about authorization levels, but the stakeholders themselves need to agree on what they are.

> **TIP**
>
> Distinctions between who does the work, who makes decisions, who approves the work, who signs off on the work, and who can veto decisions need to be clarified; this is essential information for the trusted advisor.

Defining authorization levels is not always straight-forward and is usually harder and more time-consuming than we think. Distinctions between who does the work, who makes decisions, who approves the work, who signs off on the work, and who can veto decisions need to be clarified. Plus, the team needs to define what accountability really means to them. By clarifying the nuances between role, responsibility, and accountability, we not only lower the risk of confusion and conflict, but we make it easier as trusted advisors to provide the appropriate advice to the appropriate stakeholders.

In addition, it may be helpful to assign approval levels for different aspects of project work. Let's consider an example. On a project to create a new pricing system for a retailer, David, a business analyst, might plan several requirements elicitation events. He has gotten agreement that if there are fewer than five SMEs, he can decide who to invite. If there are between five and ten participants, David will recommend invitees to a client manager, who may add participants and/or veto others. If there are more than ten invitees, the decision on who needs to participate comes from the sponsor, who will invite the participants. Such a process minimizes the risk of excess bureaucracy and unnecessary approvals. And it helps us as influencers to approach the appropriate stakeholders.

Responsibility Assignment Matrix

RACI. One way to clarify stakeholder influence is by using a responsibility assignment matrix. There are several different matrices that help with this clarification. One such matrix is **RACI**, which helps teams understand their level of authority on projects.

DOWNLOADABLE TEMPLATE

Our website has a downloadable template to help you build your own RACI charts. RACI stands for:

R = Responsibility (who does the work).

A = Accountable (who approves, makes the decision, signs off).

C = Consults with (who we need to consult with and get input from).

I = Inform (who we need to inform after the work is done).

RACI models can be developed for a project (very high level), a project phase, an activity or task, or a deliverable. In general, it is preferable if there is only one accountable person. If multiple people are accountable, the RACI may need to be decomposed into a lower level.

TIP

If there are several approvers in a RACI, the project may need to be decomposed into phases, deliverables, or activities to reach a point where there is only one person accountable for the work.

If the team completes a RACI for a project and finds there are several approvers, the project may need to be decomposed into phases, deliverables, or activities to reach a point where there is only one person accountable for the work. In that case, the high-level RACI diagrams can be kept for a bigger picture of responsibilities. Remember that it is the role and the authority level that is important. In general, it is best not to include either the title of the person or a specific person's name on the matrix.

The following model shows examples of a RACI model for both one deliverable and for an activity within a deliverable. RACIs can also be used for an entire small project or simple project phase. The more components and complexity, the more it will need to be decomposed to a lower level. We are showing two formats below, either of which can be used with deliverables and activities.

RACI for Requirements Package				
Role	Responsible	Accountable	Consult With	Inform
Sponsor		X		
Business SME			X	
Business Analyst	X			
Project Manager			X	X
Technical SME				X
Testing			X	

TABLE 6: Deliverable-Based RACI Example

Activity RACI						
Activity	**Sponsor**	**Business SME**	**Technical SME**	**BA**	**PM**	**QA**
Activity 1	A	R		R	C	C
Activity 2	A	R	C	R		I
Activity 3	I	R, A		R	C	C
Activity 4		R, A		R		I
Activity 5	A	R	I	R		I

TABLE 7: Activity-Based RACI Example – One Deliverable

As a final note, RACI also works well for ongoing operational work. For example, we used it to clarify roles and responsibilities with an outside marketing firm. It helped to clarify roles and defined approval levels for various outputs so that we knew how they would influence us and vice versa.

3. Categorize Stakeholders

In order to influence stakeholders, we need to know the specific stakeholders who will fulfill various roles. If a key stakeholder's input is missed, it is unlikely that the end-product will meet expectations.

Therefore, to do the right thing for the organization, we need to influence the right stakeholders to participate on the project. In other words, we need to identify the correct stakeholders who will help us prepare for our influencing events.

Who should create the stakeholder list? It is often the task of the project manager. If the project manager has already created an initial stakeholder register/list, the business analyst will want to confirm it and recommend changes as needed.

If the project manager has not yet created a stakeholder list, then the business analyst can develop one for the business analysis effort and provide this information to the project manager for input into the overall project documentation.

Lack of Ownership

One of the things the trusted advisor needs to do is to ensure that the business owns the end result of the project. Not having the right business SMEs involved in projects is one of the most frequent complaints we get from our workshop participants. It is common for project teams to express frustration because clients are not available to them. Because of their ongoing job duties, clients do not always have time for elicitation events. On some projects, it seems like the more knowledgeable an SME is, the less time they can devote. Such lack of participation points out several things:

> **TIP**
>
> Lack of ownership can be a symptom of resistance to the project or to the end-product. We need to influence stakeholders to take ownership of their own products.

The clients take little or no ownership for the end result of the project. The ownership of the end-product then falls on the business analyst or project manager. There is a direct correlation between availability and ownership, and without one, the other rarely exists.

The sponsor may be disengaged. On some projects, sponsors approve projects and then disengage, leaving the burden of the decisions to the SMEs, project manager, or business analyst. If the sponsor does not communicate the importance of the end-product to the SMEs, it is unlikely that they will want to actively participate in meetings to define the requirements for that product.

There might be miscommunication between the sponsor and the SMEs. Even if sponsors are engaged and place high importance on the end-product, they may fail to communicate the priority to the business SMEs. If the sponsor communicates the priority of the product to the project manager and business analyst but does not communicate it to the appropriate SMEs, it is unlikely that the SMEs will be fully engaged.

Sometimes business analysts define requirements themselves. With such transfer of ownership, the business analyst often takes on responsibility for the training and support as well, sometimes indefinitely.

> **TIP**
>
> We can increase the odds of successful projects by influencing appropriate stakeholders to take ownership for their part of a project.

In addition to the above points, lack of ownership can be a symptom of resistance to the project or end-product. SMEs often resist change for a variety of reasons. They may be afraid of having to learn a new product, losing their expertise, changing a comfortable business process, or even losing their jobs. Such resistance is often manifested in passive ways, such as not showing up for elicitation meetings.

A huge contributor to project and ultimately business success is the ability of project professionals to influence business SMEs to take ownership of their project and end-product. Stakeholder involvement and executive support have consistently been at or near the top of the important factor contributing to project success, according to various Standish Group reports.[5]

We can increase the odds of successful projects by influencing appropriate stakeholders to take ownership for their part of a project.

Understanding Stakeholder Communication Preferences

Another advantage of analyzing stakeholders is that it gives you a chance to reflect on and understand key stakeholders' communication preferences. Why is that important? Isn't it better to keep a consistent style of communication with all stakeholders?

> **TIP**
>
> To be influential, it is essential to understand and then match the communication style of the "influencee."

To be influential, we believe it is essential to understand and then match the communication style of the "influencee." (That's not a real word, but we'll use it anyway.) We don't mean you should mimic the speech habits or pitch or accent of the "influencee." The important thing to match is the way your stakeholder receives and transmits information.

There are two paradigms you can use to help you quickly assess your stakeholders' communication style. Both are based on psychology and communication theory. Because this is a practical book, we won't address the underlying science but instead present its application.

The two paradigms that we've used extensively include:

- Communication style inventory.
- Neuro-linguistic programming.

Communication Style Inventory

Many frameworks of personality or communication style revolve around two basic dimensions attributed to the psychologist Carl Jung. The two dimensions are the extent to which we are:

1. Task-oriented vs. people-oriented.
2. Internally-energized vs. externally-energized.

These dimensions are a continuum, and all humans utilize all the dimensions. We tend to favor and consistently communicate using a specific combination of these dimensions, as illustrated in *Figure 4* . The image is available as a download on our website.

Communication Style Analysis Model

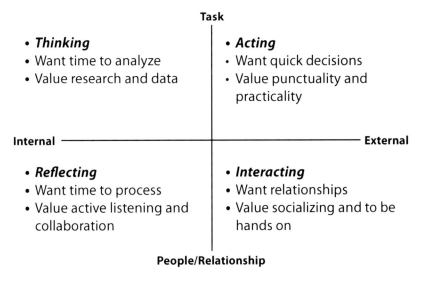

FIGURE 4: Communication Style Analysis Model

As shown in *Figure 4*, the two dimensions form four quadrants as follows:

Acting: People who have a task orientation and are externally energized. They want quick decisions and value punctuality.
Interacting: People who are externally energized and relationship-oriented. They want relationships and value socializing and hands-on involvement.
Reflecting: People who are relationship-oriented and internally energized. They want time to reflect and value active listening and collaboration.
Thinking: People who are internally energized and task-oriented. They want time to think and value data and research.

TABLE 8: Communication Styles Summary

How can we take advantage of this model to improve our ability to influence? Instead of communicating with our own standard and comfortable mode, we should practice communicating in the style of the stakeholder we wish to influence. As a general rule, people feel more comfortable communicating with and relating to others who use the same style.

The saying that "opposites attract" may apply to marriage, but in business, we have found that similar styles are preferable when trying to influence.

As we work towards becoming a trusted advisor, we can also use the communication style analysis to work on building credibility. The topic of credibility is dealt with in more detail in other parts of this book. In *Figure 5*, we summarize some tips for how to demonstrate your credibility with each of the styles.

This is important because people with different styles will perceive our credibility differently. For instance, if we spend time socializing at the beginning of meetings, the task-oriented types will be frustrated. On the other hand, if we *don't* work on relationships, the people-oriented styles will disengage and lose interest. By paying attention to and providing what is important to each style, we enhance our credibility and the perception of it.

Communication Style Analysis Model Tips

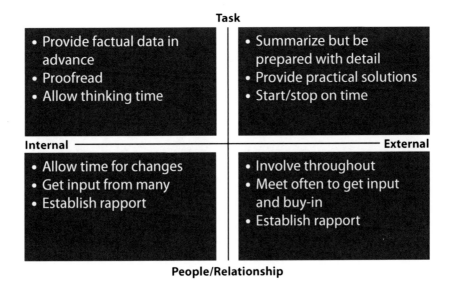

Task	
• Provide factual data in advance • Proofread • Allow thinking time	• Summarize but be prepared with detail • Provide practical solutions • Start/stop on time
Internal	**External**
• Allow time for changes • Get input from many • Establish rapport	• Involve throughout • Meet often to get input and buy-in • Establish rapport

People/Relationship

FIGURE 5: Communication Style Analysis Tips

To illustrate the importance of matching communication styles, Elizabeth learned a painful lesson while trying to influence a potential client. The situation was a sales opportunity with a stakeholder whose communication style was in the "Thinking" quadrant. She thought that her natural "Interacting" style would illustrate our engaging training approach and was determined to demonstrate it in a sales situation.

"By focusing on my own style, I missed the analytical, thinking style of the other person. When he asked 'That is all well and good. But, how well do your courses align with PMI?' I blurted out 'PM what?' (In our early days of project management training, we did not adhere as closely to PMI standards as we do now.) I was lacking in both stakeholder analysis preparation and understanding of what was important to the 'influencee.' Needless to say, I had little influence in that situation or with that prospective client."

Mirroring Styles

Speaking of sales, it is well understood that good salespeople match or "mirror" the style and posture of their prospects. If their customers talk slowly, good salespeople slow down to match them. If the prospect is animated, experienced salespeople are lively. A good salesperson sits with upright posture if the potential customer is sitting up straight.

We are not suggesting you become a carbon copy of or parrot the "influencee" by speeding up exactly when the other person does or by sitting up straight immediately after your "influencee" does. That approach is usually noticeable and often offensive. What we are suggesting is maintaining a similar, not an exact, mirroring. For example, if the person you are interacting with relaxes and slouches a bit, wait a moment or two and follow suit. If you stay erect when your "influencee" relaxes, the difference in posture can cause tension. By relaxing somewhat close in time together, the mirrored posture puts the other person more at ease and gives the impression that you are "with them" and understand them.

These responses become automatic with an experienced salesperson, and they can be learned and will become automatic for you if you practice them long enough.

It begins with awareness and develops by consciously practicing the mirroring in safe situations. We don't recommend starting your first mirroring attempt with the executive sponsor of your project! Try it out with a "safe" colleague with whom you already have a good relationship.

Here is a quick example of a potential "influencer" who did not understand the concept of mirroring and ended up not being influential. The non-influential person was a salesperson candidate of our company who spent much of the interview slouched in his chair, with his head resting on his hand. Rich, who was interviewing him, sat upright as usual and noticed the disparity in styles halfway through the interview. It felt to Rich that the candidate was condescending and not very motivated to land the job, and he didn't. He was not very influential!

Neuro-Linguistic Programming

The construct of Neuro-Linguistic Programming (NLP) is an outgrowth of studies in communication and psychotherapy and describes a useful framework we can use for categorizing stakeholder communication preferences. NLP theory describes three basic means of perceiving and learning information. NLP also helps us to understand the preferred manner in which people make decisions.

The three types are summarized in *Table 9*. Bear in mind these are generalities, and people can show preferences for more than one type. The benefit of understanding NLP comes from increasing our understanding of stakeholders and how they prefer to absorb information, learn new things, and reach decisions.

We can use these concepts to:

- Present information appropriately to increase understanding and absorption (see tips below).
- Make logical or emotional appeals when facilitating a decision.
- Help to train people according to their preferred style.

NLP Type	How People Perceive/ Decide/Learn	Tip-Off Phrases to Watch for	Tips for Presenting Information
Visual	• Visually • Logically • Reading	"I see what you mean." "I want to look into that." "Let's see what Susan says."	• Use visual images extensively • OK to use PowerPoint
Auditory	• Aurally • Gut-level • Listening	"Sounds good!" "I hear you." "Let's hear from John."	• Choose words carefully • Avoid PowerPoint
Kinesthetic	• Tacitly • Practically • Doing	"I can get my arms around that." "Let's get a hold of some data."	• Need to be hands-on to learn • Use appropriate PowerPoint

TABLE 9: Neuro-Linguistic Programming Types

Here is an example of how NLP might have helped Richard on a previous job. A peer-level manager named Mark was a burly bear of a man, who was well-respected in the organization. When he wanted something, Mark would stand in the doorway and literally not let people easily pass until he got what he wanted. His favorite expression was "I can get my arms around that."

Does that sound like a kinesthetic style? (His second-favorite expression was "sounds good." Mark had some auditory in him too.)

Had Rich recognized NLP styles, he might have done a better job of influencing Mark to get what he wanted. He might have used kinesthetic phrases, or instead of using his own preferred words and visuals, he might have used shapes or tokens to represent consultants and let Mark move them around as we discussed solutions. (Mark had control of resources that Richard wanted.) By not understanding NLP, Rich approached Mark's kinesthetic style with his own visual style, and the two styles rarely matched.

As influencers, then, we can use NLP to provide cues to help us better interact with stakeholders in a way that "looks right," "sounds right," or "feels right" to them.

> **TIP**
>
> NLP provides cues we can use to help us better interact with stakeholders in a way that "looks right," "sounds right," or "feels right" to them.

Categorization Worksheets

Once the right resources are assigned to project tasks, we need to categorize stakeholders, a process which includes developing a Stakeholder Classification Worksheet and documenting contact information on a Stakeholder Contact Worksheet. This categorization helps us see stakeholders at a glance and quickly determine not only who we need to influence but the constraints that might inhibit our ability to influence. See *Table 10* and *Table 11*.

The Stakeholder Classification Worksheet can contain any number of categories to help group stakeholders who have been assigned to projects. Particularly helpful for influencing are:

Geographic Location - This can include such things as whether or not stakeholders are colocated, national, regional, small town or big city, in a different time zone, etc. The further away stakeholders are, the harder it is to influence them. Categorizing stakeholders by geographic location can be useful for:

- Cultural awareness, when different national or regional cultures are represented, since different influence techniques work best in different cultures.
- Understanding possible attitudes towards the project or product.
- Overcoming communications barriers (language, accents, use of terminology and acronyms, pre-judging others).

Areas of Expertise - Project stakeholders typically have different areas of expertise. We may have SMEs who, for example, have facilitation expertise and who can lead elicitation workshops or are expert in using new technology or commercial software. As influencers we need to provide specific kinds of advice to stakeholders with specific expertise. For example, if we advise a business owner about databases and programming languages, it is not likely that they will follow our advice.

Technical Comfort Level - Our SMEs will probably include those who are comfortable with technology and those who may not be. This category may help us leverage their expertise and comfort with new technology and with helping to mentor and train others. Speaking of technical comfort level, Elizabeth once visited a doctor, who complained about a new system he had to use. He said it was cumbersome to use and made it hard to find the information he needed. His area of expertise was not technology, but he had had no input into the new system, which was a commercial package. A real trusted advisor would have influenced the project team to include a doctor representation on this project to automate medical records.

Internal/External to Performing Organization - It is useful to categorize stakeholders by whether or not they work for the performing organization (the performing organization being the one for whom the project is being run). External staff can include vendors, regulators, auditors, or focus/usability group participants. Trusted advisors will use different ways to influence these two groups.

Group Represented - We need to know which constituencies the SMEs represent. This category might help us identify omitted, additional, and backup SMEs. In addition, this category can be broken down further into the type of group they represent. For instance, we can have stakeholders who represent a business function or government agency with or without technical expertise, co-located or not, etc.

Number of Stakeholders Represented - We can also categorize by the number of constituents each SME represents. When SMEs represent a large number of other stakeholders, they have more influence than those representing fewer. This category is useful when looking for key influencers whom we can use to influence others.

Number of Affected Processes - The number of business processes changed as a result of a project directly impacts the lives of those who will use it, support it, train on it, sell it, answer questions about any issues with it, or interface with it in any way. Knowing which stakeholders are affected by which changed processes can be useful in numerous ways. The more processes that are changing, the greater the risk of resistance. It will be necessary, then, to focus on these stakeholder relationships in order to build trust, reduce risk, and increase influence.

Stakeholder Classification Worksheet

Name	Geo. Location	Technical Expertise	Internal or External	Group Represented	No. of SMEs	No. of Processes	No. of Systems	Org. Readiness

TABLE 10: Stakeholder Classification Worksheet

Stakeholder Contact Worksheet

Name	Group Represented	Project Role	Job Title	Dept	Email	Phone	Address

TABLE 11: Stakeholder Contact Worksheet

Number of Affected Systems - As with affected processes, this category is useful to help us understand impact. There may or may not be a correlation between the number of processes changing and the number of changing systems. For example, the development of a new system that allows various state agencies to view information on convicted criminals might cause more processes to change than a project that updates existing crime-sharing software with a new release.

Organizational Readiness Assessment - Another category, one that can be completed as more becomes known, is how likely the stakeholders are to accept the change. Understanding the stakeholders' readiness helps develop strategies for gaining acceptance.

The final step in categorizing stakeholders is to develop a contact list, which can help organize a great deal of information. Table 8 is an example of a Stakeholder Contact Worksheet, which should be customized for each project.

A stakeholder register, the output from categorizing stakeholders, consolidates information about key stakeholders, including both categorization and contact information (*PMBOK®* *Guide* - Fourth Edition, Section 10.1.3). *Tables 10 and 11* are two examples of stakeholder register worksheets, both of which are available on our website as downloadable templates.

DOWNLOADABLE TEMPLATE

4. Analyze Stakeholder Influence

As we have seen, there are a variety of ways to categorize stakeholders. As this is a book on influence, it is appropriate to discuss the influence that stakeholders are likely to have on a project. There are many models, grids, and matrices that show influence in relation to different factors. We include five of them to consider, depending on the situation.

DOWNLOADABLE TEMPLATE

a) Stakeholder Influence-Acceptance Matrix

One such grid, the Stakeholder Influence Acceptance Matrix, shows organizational influence in relation to the likely acceptance of the final outcome, as shown in *Figure 6*. It is available on our website as a downloadable template. Use this grid if you feel there is resistance to the product or the project or potential sabotage.

- **High Acceptance/High Influence – Champions**. These people are typically project sponsors and other executives who have a vested interest in a project's outcome. They often have positional and reward authority but can have personal or expert power instead of or in addition to authority.

- **Low Acceptance/High Influence – Saboteurs**. We call these individuals saboteurs because they can potentially sabotage your project or block a recommendation due to their influence. If these people have not bought into your initiatives, they can raise issues and concerns that may delay or even halt your work.

- **High Acceptance/Low Influence – The Faithful**. These types of people are similar to Champions by accepting or perhaps even pushing for the change your project or recommendation might bring about. What differentiates them is the level of influence they carry in the organization. We need to keep in touch with them enough to monitor whether they continue to be accepting or not. They can provide valuable support.

- **Low Acceptance/Low Influence – Expected Opposition**. Some individuals are resistant to change, which we expect on most projects. Our advice is to move forward knowing there will be opposition and to learn the reasons for the opposition. However, we don't advise spending as much time on this category's concerns as with the Saboteurs. Time spent with Saboteurs will increase your influence far more than time spent with the Expected Opposition.

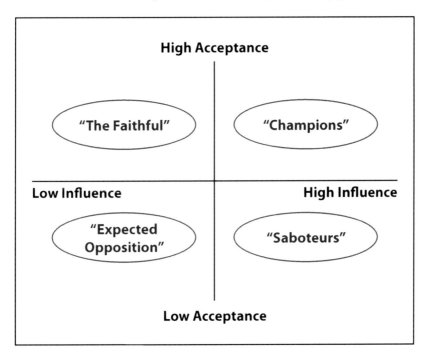

FIGURE 6: Stakeholder Influence-Acceptance Matrix

The influence analysis grid is most useful to help categorize the Champions and Saboteurs for your recommendation or project. Place their names in the grid according to their relative acceptance/influence. It can help prioritize the time we spend maintaining relationships on our projects. The Saboteur category of stakeholder may be the most important. As humans we are not typically drawn to those who oppose what we are doing. Yet, if these individuals or groups have sufficient influence, they can delay or derail our projects. It follows that we should devote adequate time to understand Saboteur concerns and make sure we address them.

Figure 7 lists some ideas for interacting with each category of stakeholder in the Influence Analysis Matrix.

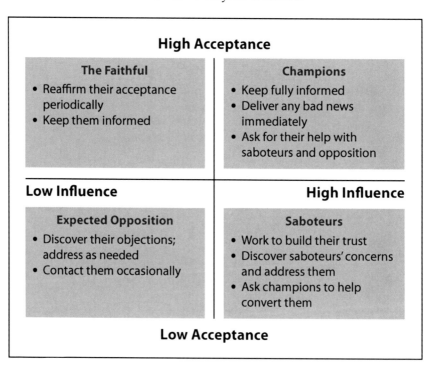

FIGURE 7: Stakeholder Influence Tips

b) Salience Model

Another model of stakeholder influence is called the Salience Model. Since appearing in *PMBOK® Guide* – Fourth Edition, the Salience Model has become a hot topic for project professionals. In a paper presented to the Academy of Management in 1997, entitled *Toward a Theory of Stakeholder Identification and Salience: Defining the Principle of Who and What Really Counts,*[6] Mitchell, Agle, and Wood presented their model of stakeholder salience, or "the degree to which managers give priority to competing stakeholder claims."

Using an example of marketing for non-profit organizations, they discussed how stakeholders are identified by their possession of one or more of three salient characteristics: power, legitimacy, and urgency.

- Power: How able are they to impose their will?
- Urgency: How immediate does a response need to be?
- Legitimacy: How appropriate is the stakeholder's involvement?

It's beyond the scope of this book to discuss the ways in which power is a type of influence and legitimacy is a type of power. All three salient characteristics are important and help analyze stakeholder influence.

c) Stakeholder Risk Analysis Matrix

Another matrix is available if you need to analyze stakeholders to identify risk associated with lack of acceptance of the project, the requirements, and/or the end-product. This grid can be useful if you or your stakeholders are comfortable doing risk analysis on projects. It is also valuable if stakeholder involvement or urgency is a typical issue on your projects.

- *Low Risk:* A <u>positive attitude</u> towards the project and end-product typically has relatively low risk to things such as project management processes, business analysis work, requirements, testing, etc. This is true regardless of the level of involvement required or organizational influence. A <u>negative attitude</u> will result in a low risk to the above only if the <u>stake is low</u>: the project is of low impact to the stakeholder, the stakeholder does not have a lot of influence within the organization, and the stakeholder does not need to be involved to any extent.

- *High Risk*: There is a high risk when the stakeholder has a <u>negative attitude</u> towards project management processes, business analysis work, requirements, and/or the end-product when the stakeholder:

  a) has influence within the organization,

  b) should have a high level of involvement,

  c) has a high sense of urgency, or

  d) is impacted to a large extent by the end-product or by project work.

Even if the <u>attitude is positive</u>, there is still risk when a high level of involvement is required and the stakeholder will be highly impacted and has a low sense of urgency.

Completing a stakeholder risk analysis matrix (see *Table 12)* is most valuable for trusted advisors to help explain these nuances in ways that help sponsors understand why certain resources present more or less risk to the project. It is also useful because it facilitates discussions with the sponsors, SMEs, and other project stakeholders and team members in a variety of ways.

By emphasizing the risks of having or not having certain SMEs involved in requirements elicitation, business clients can more easily understand which resources will be the most effective. A stakeholder risk analysis grid, then, provides supporting detail for recommendations on having the right SMEs involved.

It is also useful to project managers for developing the staffing plan, which charts which stakeholders come on to and leave the project, when their tasks begin and end, and the effort that will be required. PMs will be better prepared to influence resource managers.

It is valuable for recognizing potential sources of risks so that mitigation plans can be put in place.

Table 12 uses the following terms:

- *Risk* includes both the probability of and negative impact to the outcome of the project and the end-product, if these factors are aligned as shown in the grid.
- *Attitude* refers to the attitude towards the project in general, the time frame, the cost, the end-product, and/or the other stakeholders.
- *Influence* was defined in Chapter 1. Influence in this context refers to the way stakeholders react to the project, product, project management, or business analysis. Anyone on the project can use interpersonal skills to have a positive or negative effect on others.

TIP

When there is a mismatch between stakeholder perception and what is needed on the project, we need to influence stakeholders concerning why their involvement is required on the project.

- *Sense of urgency* indicates how involved the stakeholder wants to be. Stakeholders who are not available for elicitation events, for project and requirements reviews and inspections, or for testing the final product do not have a sense of urgency. If their involvement is required and they have little sense of urgency, there is risk of a negative outcome.

- *Level of involvement* is the amount of time that a stakeholder is needed to be available during a project. If stakeholders are not involved in a project, they will not devote the time needed to elicit and validate their requirements or to test the end-product. Lack of involvement leads to risk and, if not mitigated, can result in end-products that don't meet business needs.

- *Impact* refers to how much stakeholders will be affected by either the project work or by the change caused by implementing the end-result. There is usually a close relationship between the impact of the change with the level of involvement needed and the related sense of urgency.

Table 12 is an example of a stakeholder risk analysis matrix. There is no downloadable template for this, as it is a reference table and does not change.

If Attitude:	*and* Influence	Stake: Involvement	Urgency	Impact	Then Risk:
Positive	x	High	Low	High	High
Positive	x	High	High	x	Low
Negative	x	High	High	High	High
Negative	Low	Low	Low	Low	Low

* Note: X = N/A

TABLE 12: Stakeholder Risk Analysis Matrix

In sum, the above examples and grid show the importance of attitude on the outcome of the project and the final product. Now let's focus on the effect of stakeholder influence on the outcome of projects.

d) Stakeholder Influence Analysis Matrix

Another way to analyze stakeholders is to categorize them by the influence they have in the organization, formal or informal, compared to what we need during projects. *Table 13* is an example of such a matrix, which is available on our website as a downloadable template. Notice the Plan column is waiting to be completed and is used to record your plan for how to deal with the various stakeholders. The topic of planning your stakeholder approach is covered later in this section.

DOWNLOADABLE TEMPLATE

Stakeholder Influence Analysis Matrix					
Stakeholder	Project Role	Organizational Influence	Influence Required	Influence on Project	Plan
Wanda Jones	Sponsor	High positional/ high personal	High	Engaged	
Brian Smith	SME	Low positional/ negative	High	Will tend to create conflict	
Josh Meyer	Developer	Low positional/ high expert	High	May act creatively	

TABLE 13: Stakeholder Influence Analysis Matrix

In the above example, with Wanda, you may not need to do anything except keep her informed of issues and progress. With Brian, who will create conflict, you could try meeting individually with him to understand his concerns and address them. (But, you may want to spend limited time with him due to low positional influence.) Josh is someone you need to have involved in the project because of his expertise. Frequent reviews of his work may be needed to keep his "creativity" to a minimum.

e) Power/Interest Grid

Yet another way to analyze both the stake and the power of key stakeholders is called a Power/Interest Grid. Use this grid to help you analyze stakeholders if you are concerned about how their power and interest (or lack thereof) affects your project.

Figure 8 provides an example:

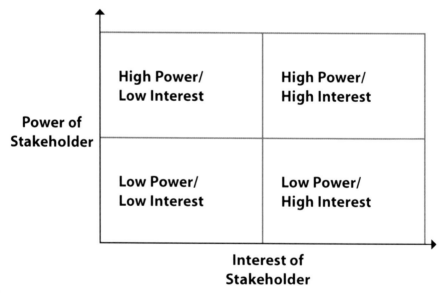

FIGURE 8: Power/Interest Grid

The Power/Interest Grid has four quadrants. As you categorize your stakeholders in this grid, think in terms of their relative positional power in the organization as well as the level of concern the stakeholders have about the final product. Also analyze your stakeholders' level of interest in the project. The impact to them is another way to categorize stakeholder interest. *Table 14* provides an example of groups of stakeholders who might be included in the Power/Interest Grid.

Power/Interest	Stakeholder Groups
High power/low interest	Executives not directly sponsoring the project.
Low power/low interest	Business analysts and project managers on other projects, as well as other business units not directly affected by the effort.
High power/high interest	Champions, such as sponsors.
Low power/high interest	Key SMEs and the groups they represent.

TABLE 14: Power/Interest Groups

5. Plan Approach to Maximize Support

The final process in stakeholder analysis is to develop a plan to maximize their support. The *PMBOK Guide®* – Fourth Edition calls this the Stakeholder Management Strategy, which is an output of the task "Identify Stakeholders" in the Project Communications Knowledge Areas (*PMBOK® Guide*, Section 10.1).[7] The plan should include the results of the stakeholder analysis, with specific actions that will be taken to influence a positive outcome.

Figure 9 and *Table 15* summarize ways to gain support and buy-in with each stakeholder category.

	High Power/Low Interest	High Power/High Interest
Power of Stakeholder	• Keep satisfied • Leverage champions to help manage their issues	• Build trust • Keep informed of progress and issues • Keep satisfied • Advise and recommend
	Low Power/Low Interest	**Low Power/High Interest**
	• Check in periodically • Discuss areas of overlap • Keep informed of issues	• Build trust • Get them involved • Keep them involved • Raise their issues • Advise and recommend

Interest of Stakeholder

FIGURE 9: Power/Interest Grid Tips

Stakeholder Influence Analysis Matrix				
Stakeholder	**Project Role**	**Organizational Influence**	**Columns omitted for space reasons**	**Plan**
Wanda Jones	Sponsor	High positional/ high personal		None
Brian Smith	SME	Low positional/ negative		Hold one-on-ones Reinforce rules Assigned seating
Josh Meyer	Developer	Low positional/ high expert		Hold one-on-ones Review output carefully

TABLE 15: Stakeholder Influence Analysis Matrix With Plan

There are numerous ways to build support with stakeholders, which help both with preparation and with building trust, two of the three components of the influencing formula. Here is a list of strategies to help you gain support with your stakeholders:

- *Leverage champions.* Look to the sponsor to articulate how the project objectives are aligned with the business objectives and strategic direction of the organization, as well as the benefits of the end-product.
- *Ensure all SMEs understand how the project solves a real business problem* and aligns with the organization's strategic direction and business objectives.
- *Ensure all SMEs know how the process and end-product will benefit them.* This is often called the WIIFM, or "what's in it for me."
- Even better is what we call "WIIFO," or "what's in it for the organization." For more on WIIFM and WIIFO, see Chapter 8.
- *Encourage input early and often.* Meet frequently. Do one-on-ones before and after facilitated workshops to ensure understanding of issues and requirements.
- *Spend time understanding the SMEs' issues and pressures.* If possible, spend time in their areas, using their systems, following their processes.
- *Spend time getting to know your SMEs.* Use appropriate influencing types suggested in the previous chapter, such as networking and planting seeds. Discuss topics of interest to them that are not related to work or the project. This also helps build their trust.

✑ *Summary*

- .This chapter covered five key stakeholder analysis tasks and associated tools, including identifying required roles, defining roles and authorization levels, categorizing stakeholders, analyzing stakeholder influence, and planning strategies for gaining stakeholder support.

- We presented many tools in this chapter to help understand, categorize, and analyze stakeholders as part of the influencing formula preparation phase. Not all are needed on every effort, and there may be some you prefer over others. (Each of the authors has different favorites.)

- To help sort through the many choices, *Table 16* provides a summary and some guidance.

1   Stephen Covey. The Seven Habits of Highly Effective People. (New York: Free Press, 2004), 235.

2   Project Management Institute. A Guide to the Project Management Body of Knowledge (PMBOK® Guide), 4th ed. (Newtown Square, PA: Project Management Institute, 2008), Glossary.

3   Project Management Institute. A Guide to the Project Management Body of Knowledge (PMBOK® Guide), 4th ed. (Newtown Square, PA: Project Management Institute, 2008), Section 1.4.4 and 1.6, the role of the Project Manager.

4   IIBA and Kevin Brennan. A Guide to the Business Analysis Body of Knowledge® (BABOK® Guide), 2nd ed. West Valley City, UT: Waking Lion Press, 2009. 6.

5   PM Hut. "My Theory Why IT Projects Fail," PM Hut - The Project Management Hut, accessed August 04, 2012, http://www.pmhut.com/my-theory-on-why-it-projects-fail

6   R.K. Mitchell, B.R. Agle and D.J. Wood, "Toward a Theory of Stakeholder Identification and Salience: Defining the Principle of Who And What Really Counts," Academy of Management Review 22(4) (1997): 854

7   Project Management Institute. A Guide to the Project Management Body of Knowledge (PMBOK® Guide), 4th ed. Appendix G5, (Newtown Square, PA: Project Management Institute, 2008), 246.

Summary of Stakeholder Analysis Tools

Tool	Type	Purpose	Tips for Usage
RACI	Responsibility Assignment Matrix	Clarify key roles and responsibilities, including authority for approvals and sign-offs.	Useful for all project types and sizes. Discover decision-makers who you need to influence.
Communication Style Inventory	Categorize people as: Acting, Interacting, Reflecting, or Thinking	Understand whether stakeholders are people- or task-oriented and externally- or internally-energized.	Build credibility by catering to specific styles. Refer to tips in text.
Neuro-Linguistic Programming (NLP)	Categorize people as: Visual, Auditory, or Kinesthetic	Understand how stakeholders absorb, learn, and decide on information. Communicate in language and methods most comfortable to specific stakeholders.	Use language and phrases familiar to stakeholders. Present information and training in formats matching NLP style.
Mirroring	Style matching	Be aware of behavior of the person you are attempting to influence; not a tool, but a good practice.	Don't be a parrot or robot. Do mirroring in general ways. Practice this with familiar stakeholders first.

Summary of Stakeholder Analysis Tools			
Tool	**Type**	**Purpose**	**Tips for Usage**
Stakeholder Classification Worksheet	Group stakeholders by key categories to help manage large groups and ensure compete requirements	Group according to: • Geographic location • Areas of expertise • Technical comfort level • Internal/external to performing organization • Group represented • Number of stakeholders represented • Number of affected processes • Number of affected systems • Organizational readiness assessment	Not needed on smaller projects. Cultural or language issues will affect your ability to influence. The larger the groups represented, the greater the impact to them. The more processes change, the greater the need for getting stakeholder input.

Summary of Stakeholder Analysis Tools

Tool	Type	Purpose	Tips for Usage
Stakeholder Contact Worksheet	Listing of stakeholders with contact information	Useful to keep in contact with stakeholders and to track the groups they belong to and their role on a project or in the organization.	Use electronic tools where possible.
Stakeholder Influence-Acceptance Grid	Influence Analysis	Shows organizational influence in relation to the likely acceptance of the final outcome.	Use this to identify champions and saboteurs and create strategies to be able to influence them. With saboteurs, work on building their trust, discover their concerns, and leverage champions to convert them.
Salience Model	Influence Analysis	Categorize stakeholder influence by these characteristics: • Power • Legitimacy • Urgency	Salience helps determine and influence priorities.

Summary of Stakeholder Analysis Tools

Tool	Type	Purpose	Tips for Usage
Stakeholder Risk Analysis Grid	Influence Analysis	Analyze stakeholders to identify risk associated with lack of acceptance of the project, the requirements, and/or the end-product.	A positive attitude towards the project and end-product typically has relatively low risk. A negative attitude towards the project or product increases risk unless involvement, urgency, and impact are all low.
Stakeholder Influence Analysis Matrix	Influence Analysis	Categorize stakeholders by the influence they have in the organization compared to what we need during projects.	Assess organization influence by judging the positional and personal "power" of key stakeholders. Compare influence needed vs. actual project influence. Create a mitigation plan to fill the gap.

Summary of Stakeholder Analysis Tools		
Tool	**Type**	**Purpose**	**Tips for Usage**
Power/Interest Grid	Influence Analysis	Analyzes both the stake involved (i.e., interest) and the power of key stakeholders.	Power: relative to the organization (i.e., positional). See details for tips on dealing with each group. Pay most attention to High Interest and work to build their trust.

TABLE 16: Stakeholder Analysis Tools Summary

06 Influential Consulting Skills

"Every stakeholder group within the industry has strong thoughts and ideas about what's in the best interest of their group, as one would expect them to. Our concern is what's in the best interest of the entire system."

DANNY DAVIS

U.S. POLITICIAN

Previously we saw the importance of preparation as one of the main ingredients of the influencing formula. We also explored steps in preparation, namely to choose appropriate influencing techniques and analyze the stakeholders that we need to influence.

Now we turn to a major preparation technique, that of using consulting skills. It is one of the most effective and available means that project professionals have for influencing without authority and for becoming the trusted advisor of our business partners.

We were trained as internal management consultants by Peat, Marwick, and Mitchell Company (now part of KPMG Consulting). We reviewed operating departments, documented our findings of problems and opportunities, and made recommendations to executives about what to improve. This was a powerful model for influencing both management and the operating departments on things they needed to change.

Today our preferred consulting approach goes by the acronym SARIE. You will not be sorry to use this method for guiding your consulting efforts. Sorry, we couldn't resist a bad pun.

The acronym SARIE stands for:

S – Situation: *Understanding the business need*

A – Analysis: *Analyzing the business need (ask questions, determine impacts and alternatives)*

R – Recommendation: *Recommending an appropriate course of action*

I – Implementation: *Advising how to implement the recommendations*

E – Evaluation: *Helping to evaluate how well the business need was satisfied*

Figure 10 below shows a pictorial view of how SARIE flows. It assumes that influencers are consultants or trusted advisors to the business leaders and sponsors.

As trusted advisors, we need to recommend solutions that help the organization achieve its goals. The trusted advisor should articulate and analyze the current situation in order to be able to recommend a solution to the business problems or the best way to seize an opportunity.

FIGURE 10: SARIE Consulting Process

As business issues and opportunities are specified by business leaders/sponsors, the SARIE approach calls for us to respond by defining the business problem or opportunity. Too often, project professionals start planning a project to implement the request from the business instead of getting a clear definition of the situation. This is sometimes called "jumping to a solution."

After working to discover the business situation, we need to get agreement on it. A great question to understand the business need early on and to prevent jumping to solutions is to ask stakeholders: **"What business problem are we trying to solve?"** We should get to the root causes of the problem or determine the important drivers of an opportunity. "Root-cause analysis" is the main focus of the analysis stage. It breaks the situation

TIP

A great question to understand the business need early on and to prevent jumping to solutions is to ask stakeholders: "What business problem are we trying to solve?"

down into small enough pieces to be able to confidently know the cause and to recommend solutions to alleviate the problem or take advantage of the opportunity.

But I Don't Have Time to Consult!

Understandably, if you have an impatient sponsor and a tight deadline, a consultative approach may seem impractical or even impossible. You might hear the same types of messages we have heard from executives:

- "I don't want you to spend too much time in requirements meetings—the application has to be up and running by (*insert arbitrary-sounding date*)."
- "I've already told you what we need. That's why we bought the package we did!"
- "We can install the software now and customize it later."

What our experience has shown, and anecdotally the experience of our colleagues and customers, is that when we jump to solutions, we often fix the symptom and not the underlying issues. Those issues and factors don't tend to go away, causing additional rework and expense later. Worst of all is the ongoing pain and cost of living with a problem that isn't solved.

As an example, the Jefferson Memorial in Washington, DC, had a problem. The paint was wearing out much more often than it should and needed frequent repainting. A reactive, non-consultative approach would be to find better quality paint or to apply multiple coats of paint to solve the problem. But, by doing root-cause analysis, it was discovered that the reason for repainting was caused by frequent power-washing of the monument.

Why was so much power washing needed? Well, because of bug droppings, of all things, and consequently the monument was getting unsightly in the summer. By delving deeper, the reason the bugs were so prevalent was caused by lighting of the monument at dusk. The bugs were attracted to the light at dusk, but not before or afterwards.

By getting down to the root cause, a practical and effective solution was found: turn on the lights later, after dusk, when the bugs were less active. By delaying the lighting of the monument a short time, the bugs stopped swarming it, they left far fewer droppings, and the paint did not deteriorate from over-frequent washings. By determining the root cause and solving it, the team saved countless future dollars by not re-painting as frequently. They also decreased the number of power-washings needed and saved needless wear-and-tear of the monument, not to mention savings of electricity and other resources.

Now let's examine each part of SARIE, step-by-step.

Situation

It is important to have the context of the current situation before considering a solution. The current situation is sometimes known as the "as-is," and the solution represents the "to-be" state. The solution should address the limitations of the current situation. For example, if there is a new regulation, the situation should describe the ways the business technology cannot handle the new regulation. The solution would then describe how to incorporate the new regulation with both business and technical changes (if applicable).

> **TIP**
>
> Remember to be careful how you ask "Why?" We are not prosecuting attorneys questioning a suspect, demanding "Why?!" Work on your "consultative questioning" skills and always be diplomatic.

Situation Statement

The "S" part of SARIE is best summarized with something known as a Situation Statement. These are often referred to as "problem statements," but that suggests a narrower use. The word "situation" does a better job of covering both problems and opportunities.

The components of a complete situation statement include these three parts:

- Situation of "a"
- Has the Effect of "b"
- With the Impact of "c"

The <u>situation</u> portion of the statement is the current problem or opportunity. The <u>effect</u> shows how the situation matters to the organization. The <u>impact</u> explains the extent or relative size of the problem. When used properly, it guides the scope and type of solution to address the situation.

In fact, by properly framing a situation statement, you might find that something is perceived as a problem only because of the way it has been framed in the past. Edward De Bono, the 6 Hats Thinking guru, describes it this way: "Sometimes the situation is only a problem because it is looked at in a certain way. Looked at in another way, the right course of action may be so obvious that the problem no longer exists."[1]

We find this often to be true when the lack of a function or capability is viewed as a problem. For example, in our company we lack an affiliate management system. On the surface, this seems like a problem. By stating this in the following way, the problem lessens and the course of action is more obvious.

Here are two ways to frame the situation:

INITIAL THOUGHT

"We don't have an affiliate management system and therefore can't sign up new affiliates. It means we are losing potential revenue of $X per year."

REVISED THOUGHT

"Our current manual method of managing affiliates and tracking their referrals means we must use limited methods of tracking referrals, such as using access codes and custom links. We estimate we are losing potential revenues of $X per year that could be partially recouped.

By the way, at the time of writing, we are acting on the above situation for a short-term fix and working on adopting an automated solution for the long term.

Example Situation Statement

Let's look at an example for a fictitious company, Speedy Mortgage. Business leaders might be upset about the length of time it takes Speedy to process a new or refinanced loan. They may "lead by solution" and launch an initiative to install a new mortgage processing software package.

Suppose you are a business analyst or project manager assigned to the project to install the new system. Do you go straight to the project objectives and deliverables and figure out the best way to install the package? An influencer would first work to understand the business need behind such a request. The Situation Statement is an ideal way to get started. Here is what you might come up with of any problem.

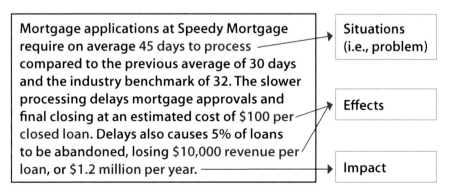

FIGURE 11: Example Situation Statement

It tells us that there is a **problem** with slow mortgage processing (45 days compared with 30-32). It has substantial **effects**, namely delayed approvals and closing of loans that cost the company money. It also tells us that there is a significant **impact**, potentially losing over one million dollars annually.

Analysis

In the analysis phase, we need to understand the root cause of the problem. We also need to know how severe the problem is or, for an opportunity situation, the size of the opportunity. In other words, how much pain is the problem causing or how much gain will the opportunity bring? In short, the "A" part of SARIE fleshes out the "as-is" part of the business issue you are addressing. We will address the root cause first.

> **TIP**
>
> Think of the Analysis phase of SARIE as finding the pain or gain of a situation.

Following is a list of several tools that are effective at helping to determine the root cause of a situation. They are fairly common, and you will recognize some or all of them.

We recommend you start with these first four basic methods because they work best with preliminary, open-ended questions. For example, "help me understand why the problem is happening."

a) Five "Whys" – Ask up to five times why the problem is happening to get to the root cause. Each time you get an answer, probe deeper as to why each successive layer is occurring. Usually, by the time you have asked five progressively deeper "why" questions, you will get to the root cause. Our earlier example about the Jefferson Memorial is an example that used this technique to probe until the cause of the lighting that attracted bugs was discovered.

b) Mind Maps – Mind maps start with a problem and branch out to find causes and sub-causes. It focuses on a central issue and works well in conjunction with the "five whys" to go deeper and deeper. See *Figure 12* for an example.

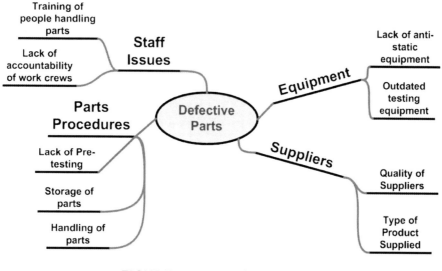

FIGURE 12: Example Mind Map

Mind maps are a visual way to capture complex ideas using key words. They are based on research that found students who took notes with key words were more efficient and remembered more information than those who recorded exact text. It is a divergent thinking way of recording key words linked together to represent how the topic, issue, or problem is perceived and inter-connected.[2]

Even though it is a visual way of recording, a mind map can be easily converted to a linear outline for a report or presentation.

Applied to consulting, mind maps can be effectively used to probe deeper and deeper into root causes of problems. They help facilitate recording of relevant factors that may be causing a problem or could contribute to an opportunity. They allow ideas to be coherently recorded as they occur, which can be effective to help stay organized and not impede the brainstorming process.

TIP

Mind maps help to:
- Probe deeper and deeper
- Facilitate recording relevant factors
- Coherently record ideas
- Keep brainstorming organized.

Constructing a Mind Map

The basic steps in creating a mind map are:

1. Select the problem or topic and draw it in the middle of the map with an oval or rectangle around it. The shape is arbitrary, so feel free to substitute other shapes. Label the problem with a meaningful name, such as "Defective Parts". See *Figure 13* for a structure to use.
2. Identify a major factor that represents a cause of the problem or is a potential driver of an opportunity. Mind maps work well for either type. Label each factor with a brief name, such as Equipment or Staff.
3. Identify sub-causes of the factor and link the sub-causes and major factor back to the main topic. Name each of these sub-causes with a meaningful, brief name, such as Quality of Suppliers.

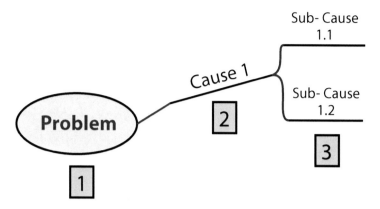

FIGURE 13: Mind Map Steps 1-3

4. Probe for subsets of the cause and link them as sub-causes to their related "parent." It may be cumbersome to go five levels deep, so only go as deep as you feel is needed or is practical. See *Figure 14*.

5. As new major factors or causes occur, link them to the main topic wherever there is room. Mind maps adapt to the flow of ideas by easily adding new factors, causes, and sub-causes as they occur.

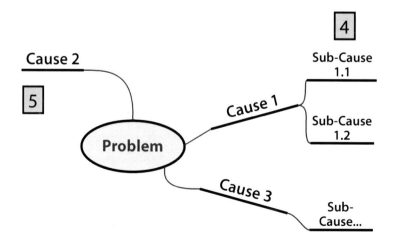

FIGURE 14: Mind Map Steps 4-5

6. Repeat steps 3-5 as new causes are identified, as shown in *Figure 15*, which is three levels deep. A mind map can easily become wavy and detailed but is visually intuitive and easy to follow.

7. If you feel your map is overly crowded or awkward, you can easily convert it to an outline. Mindmapping software, such as MindJet®, can help you do the conversion with the click of a button. Software such as Microsoft Visio® or PowerPoint® requires you to convert your maps to outlines manually, which is not a difficult process.

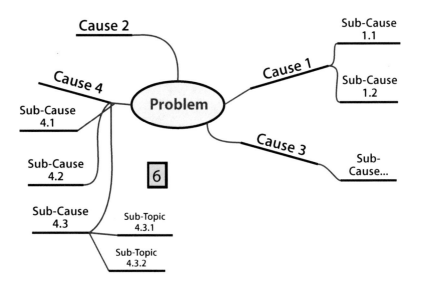

FIGURE 15: Mind Map Steps 6-7

c) Fishbone Diagrams – These are used to look for the root causes of problems using standard categories (vs. the Mind Map, which is more free-form). They are visual diagrams meant to explore a problem or opportunity at a high level, using a small number of cause

DOWNLOADABLE TEMPLATE

categories. See *Figure 16* for an example. Check our website for a downloadable template.

Typical categories include the following, depending on the type of environment you are analyzing. We advise to always include a People category because people are often part of any problem.

Production Environment	Service Environment
Equipment	Policy
Methods	Processes
Materials	Place
Measurements	Patron/customer
Environment	Systems
People	People

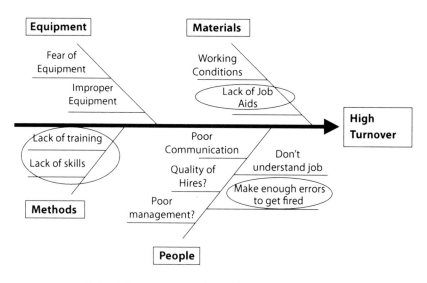

FIGURE 16: Example Fishbone Diagram

Constructing a Fishbone Diagram

Following are the basic steps to create a Fishbone Diagram. Refer to *Figure 17* for a diagram illustrating the steps.

1. Create a Situation/Problem statement for the issue to be analyzed, and place it on the right side of the diagram, such as "High Turnover" in *Figure 16* and "Late Reports" in *Figure 17*.

2. Draw the "backbone" and "ribs." Leave enough room to show at least four "ribs."

3. Decide on the major factor categories that may affect the situation. These form the major categories of causes of the problem, such as People, Methods, Equipment, etc.

4. For each category, ask what in the category may be causing the effect. For example, "Could materials be the cause of late reports, and why?" If a reasonable cause can be determined, write it down. Don't be overly critical—you are not *concluding* they are causes but identifying potential causes to study further. Like mind maps, fishbone diagrams are excellent brainstorming tools.

5. If a cause is complex enough to do a fishbone diagram, it will usually have sub-causes. Label those too. The diagram becomes overly complex if you go too deeply, so we advise keeping a fishbone diagram to two or three levels at most.

> **TIP**
>
> You can find plenty of free templates for fishbone diagrams on the Internet. Do a Google search on "Fishbone Diagrams" and also check out the Microsoft Office® template downloads. See Appendix B for free downloadable templates that we supply.

6. When done, look for clusters of causes and patterns, especially repeated causes. Circle the ones that you feel merit further investigation. These are useful items to measure, model, or otherwise study in more detail and are more likely to lead you to the root cause of the situation. "Win98" and "Shortage of Staff" below are examples of key causes.

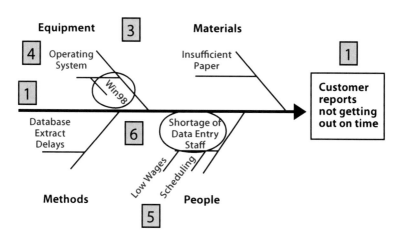

FIGURE 17: Constructing a Fishbone Diagram

d) Process Diagrams – This method helps us to look for causes of process problems and gaps in capabilities, including missing capabilities. They are a popular tool and help stakeholders think concretely about their business and its possible problems. See *Figure 18* for an example.

For each step in a process, ask, "How might this step contribute to the problem?" Note the causes on the diagram as branches from the appropriate process step as in the example. Break each potential cause into sub-causes if the cause is complex enough.

It is tempting to think about how to improve the current process as you analyze each step, but process improvement will distract you from finding the root cause of the overall problem. The problem box on the right of the diagram will remind you and your team of the overall problem that needs to be solved. It is usually more effective to work on process improvement later as a second iteration of analyzing the process.

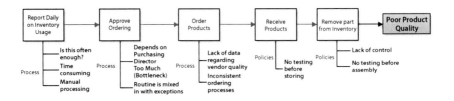

FIGURE 18: Example Process Diagram

Constructing a Process Diagram

Following are the basic steps for converting a process diagram into a cause-and-effect diagram. Refer to *Figure 19* for a diagram illustrating the steps.

1. Find a current model of the process being analyzed. If none exists (which is very likely), create a model.

2. Again, document a situation/problem statement for the issue to be analyzed, and place it on the right side of the diagram, such as Delayed Shipments in *Figure 19*.

3. For each step of the process, ask, "How does the given step contribute to the problem?"

4. There may be one or more categories that contribute to the problem. Use the common categories from the fishbone diagram as noted above to guide you. The example shows "Process" and "Policies" categories.

5. For each category, there may be none, one, or more sub-
causes that contribute. Note them on the diagram. Break
these sub-causes down further as the problem dictates.
Focus on any repeated issues and the causes/sub-causes
that appear to have the largest impact.

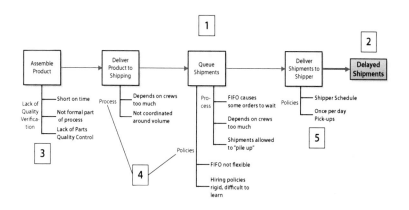

FIGURE 19: Root Causes in a Process Diagram

Getting Deeper Into the Root Cause

Once you have filtered the most likely
root causes, it's time to discover more
details about those areas. It might
be to measure critical aspects of a
problem or to get detailed measures
to discover how severe the problem

TIP

Look for the causes
that create the most
effects, and those are
the ones to fix first.

actually is. The previous techniques often suggest the measures
and specific areas to follow up on. Here are three of our favorite
techniques for measuring relevant details to help you better
understand and pinpoint the root cause.

a) Interrelationship Diagrams are a special kind of cause-and-effect diagram. They look at the causes uncovered by fishbone diagrams and mind maps and "inter-relate" them. Quite often, problems get convoluted over time and don't have one distinct cause. And, many factors can be causes of other factors that contribute to the problem.

Look for the causes that create the most effects, and fix those first. In the example diagram in *Figure 20*, the numbers "x, y" mean that a given factor has resulted x number of times in the relationship, and the factor has been a cause of other factors y number of times.

In the example below, "Shortage of staff" is the effect of only one other factor, namely "Low wages," but causes three other factors, "Not enough paper," "Database extract delays," and "Scheduling." Some factors will have a high x, such as "Database extract delays." They are quite often symptoms and will not fix the underlying problem, so do not focus on them as much.

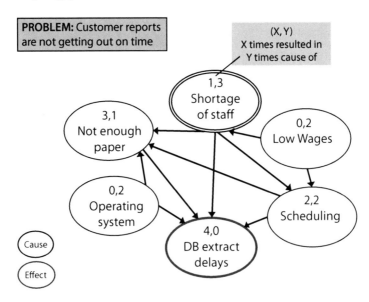

FIGURE 20: Example Interrelationship Diagram

b) Pareto Diagrams show the most significant contributors to a problem, ordered by their frequency from highest to lowest. See *Figure 21* for an example.

DOWNLOADABLE TEMPLATE

Based on the 80/20 principle, they point out quickly what should be fixed first to significantly address a business need. The Pareto Principle tells us that 80% of a problem is caused by 20% of the potential causes or factors. Many problems do not have pre-existing metrics for us to analyze. But, for problems that have metrics in the form of potential causes, Pareto charts are a must-have in any problem analysis.

TIP

80/20 rule: 80% of a problem is caused by 20% of the potential causes or factors.

In addition to problems, they can also be used to show the most significant factors or drivers of an opportunity.

The so-called "vital few" are approximately 20% of the variables that occur roughly 80% of the time. One can spot them easily on a Pareto chart when the cumulative Pareto curve reaches approximately the 80% mark, as with variables D, B, and F in *Figure 21*. The other variables are less important factors behind the problem to be solved, and are sometimes called the "trivial many." Variables A, C, E, and G below are examples of the "trivial many."

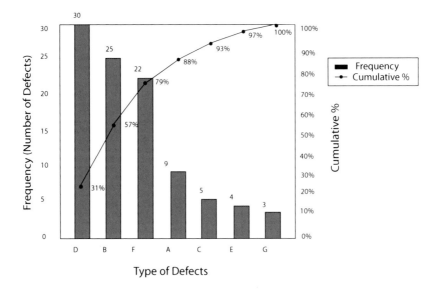

FIGURE 21: Example Pareto Diagram

As we mentioned, Pareto charts rely on data to help find the root cause of problems. We may have to capture sample data using data sheets or check sheets that end-users complete as they do their jobs to discover the key variables in the 80/20 rule.

c) Scatter Diagrams help us show trends and correlations between two sets of variables. Correlation suggests that as one variable changes, the other variable changes as well. The strength of a correlation is also revealed using this tool. Although we need to be careful that we don't infer causation from scatter diagrams, they often point us in the direction of further exploration for root cause. *Figure 22* shows a scatter diagram with clear correlation.

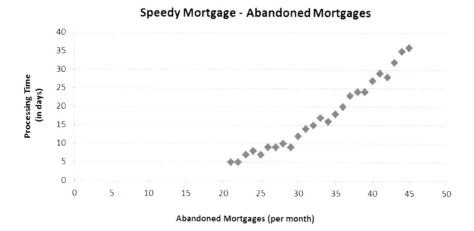

FIGURE 22: Example Scatter Diagram

The example in *Figure 22* shows clearly that the longer the delay in processing a mortgage, the more abandoned mortgages occur.

Example

Through a combination of tools, such as the Five Whys, data collection, Fishbone diagrams, Pareto analysis and process diagrams, our intrepid influencer at Speedy Mortgage determined the following from her analysis:

- Mortgage applications at Speedy Mortgage are processed by three main verification groups. These groups work sequentially, with an application processed by one group and passed to the next in turn. Each group must wait for the previous group to finish before it can begin, adding one to two additional weeks of verification time. Our study found it was routine (i.e., 80% of the time) for the second and third teams to wait up to one week for the previous team to finish its verifications.

- Underwriting information (e.g., bank statements, insurance binders, etc.) is often misplaced, requiring processors to repeat their request for it. Losing needed information happens as much as 50% of the time, and 40% of those losses can cause a one-month delay in processing. It was also found that mortgage applicants were understandably irritated by the numerous duplicate requests. In 20% of these cases, loans were abandoned.

- For 15% of the applications studied, two duplicate requests in addition to the original request were needed, causing those loans to lose their promised interest rate. In these cases, 75% of the delayed loans were later abandoned.

Recommendation

Our analysis of the situation should continue until we feel confident that we have at least 80% of the underlying root cause(s) of the problem understood. (The same consideration applies to an opportunity, only we seek to understand the main drivers of that opportunity.) Then, we can recommend appropriate solutions to address the problem or opportunity.

Optimally, our recommendations should address all the causes and factors uncovered from our analysis. By structuring our analysis point by point as we show in the previous example for Speedy Mortgage, it is easier to match the recommendations back to their corresponding causes.

Our experience has been that whenever we have gotten to the root cause of a problem, the appropriate solution seems to jump out at us. For example, our company had a problem a few years back with our website. We were updating certain web pages only to find out the changes to them got reversed and older versions re-appeared. These update issues were not frequent, but they had a large impact on our web presence.

This may sound like a simple problem, but it turned out not to be so easy to fix. Richard wanted to purchase a content management system to prevent the problem. (Hey, we are human too!) Fortunately, Elizabeth convinced him to conduct a SARIE, and we found some interesting results.

- One cause was that we had multiple authors updating pages, although they were each in charge of different pages. That was a contributing cause but not the root cause.

- By doing more Five Whys analysis, we found out that when web authors updated their separate pages, they "checked out" those pages to update, did the update, but sometimes failed to "check in" the pages. What happened was that whenever pagers were checked in, regardless of the author, the system overwrote the changes done by another author. Again, a contributing cause but not the ultimate root cause.

- Finally, we discovered the web publishing tool we used could not adequately manage the multiple authors working on the site. (See, we needed a content management system!) Actually, the root cause proved to be that multiple people had publishing ability and that was causing the overwriting of the web pages.

Once we discovered that we had multiple people doing the physical publishing, the solution became clear. Namely, we assigned one person the responsibility of web publishing. We still have multiple authors, but they funnel their changes through the publishing person. The problem was solved quickly and easily, without the expense and overhead of a content management system. Further, the problem has not re-appeared, which is the best kind of solution. We like to call this an "enduring result."

Ways to Determine Recommendations

Sometimes the recommendation(s) to a problem or opportunity are not as readily apparent. Or the political climate in your organization may not permit the optimal solution.

Here are some effective ways to generate workable recommendations:

- **Discussions with executives.** This is a wise idea in any case to help ensure buy-in and to understand any potential landmines. Recall the earlier example in which Richard was surprised by the question of "How do you know your program caused an increase in performance and that it wasn't due to hiring a higher caliber of employee?" A discussion with that executive before recommending a new program may have uncovered this concern.

- **Individual meetings** with subject matter experts (SMEs), such as process owners, managers, and staff actually doing the work. These stakeholders are important people to help us define the situation and provide insights into our root cause analysis.

- **Competitive analysis.** Quite often, competitors have already addressed the same problem or have noticed the same market opportunity. Another name for this is benchmarking. Despite the feeling that we need unique or original solutions, the reality is that organizations often copy each other. The key is to differentiate your solution. We heard a keynote presentation by Malcolm Gladwell at a PMI Congress based on his writing in which he shockingly said that Apple doesn't innovate. What they do is take other ideas and improve them enough to make them appealing. We can adapt Gladwell's idea when we do our competitive analysis to help us find workable solutions to problems and opportunities.[3] The key is to then make the solution unique to your organization by improving what competitors have done. If you work in government or in a non-profit, the same principle applies. For example, many state governments in the United States share their best practices among each other for tax collection, criminal justice, child support collections, etc.

- **Brainstorming**. This is useful when there is no clear or established kind of solution to a situation. It is most applicable when taking advantage of an opportunity or when stakeholders disagree about proposed solutions. For more on brainstorming, check out the article by Vijay Govindarajan and Jay Terwilliger titled, "Yes, You Can Brainstorm Without Groupthink," published in the Harvard Business Review in July 2012.[4]

Gaining Acceptance for Recommendations

Conduct Feasibility Analysis. If you want a practical solution that stands a higher chance of being accepted, it must be feasible. An accepted way to determine this is through feasibility analysis. That is a whole subject in itself, so let us cover the five most important factors for a feasible solution, using the TELOS framework.[5]

Telos is the Greek word for "purpose" or "goal." It also comprises a nice acronym for the five most important aspects of feasibility. By considering and analyzing these factors, we have the most important parts of feasibility analysis.

- **Technology Feasibility** - Projects are often driven by constraints of existing platforms, databases, networks, etc. You need to find out if the recommended solution is technically feasible. In addition to the traditional forms of technology, we like to include any form of technical considerations, including the skill set of people who will use the solution.

- **Economic Feasibility** - This is a preliminary cost-benefit analysis. You need to find out if the approach is affordable. Is the pay-back period quick enough? Is there sufficient return on investment (ROI)? Pay-back period and ROI are relatively easy to calculate, and both should be considered in feasibility analysis. Find out if your organization has any "hurdle rates," that is, specific levels of financial pay-back or ROI that a potential project investment must obtain. If your solution doesn't meet or exceed the hurdles, then it is not considered feasible, and you won't have much influence.

- **Legal Feasibility -** Are we violating any laws with the approach? For example, many states or countries outlaw lotteries or other forms of gambling or sweepstakes. Insurance and banking are two heavily regulated industries that affect a solution. Our case study example, Speedy Mortgage, may not be able to offer online mortgage applications in all locations. Be sure to determine if any contracts may be violated by a solution. And, even when a solution may be legal, we should also be asking "Is it ethical?" For instance, if our organization expands its sales by taking over the territory of existing affiliates or distributors, it may be unethical or may violate existing contracts and is therefore not a feasible solution.

- **Operational Feasibility -** How well does the solution meet business needs? How well does it match our high-level requirements? How easy will it be to train on, implement, sell, and support the product? For major gaps, we also like to include a recommendation for how to address them, whether it is to adjust business processes, do custom software development, or both.

- **Schedule Feasibility -** Will the recommendation accomplish what we need when we need it? This is tricky because many business leaders are impatient and feel they need their solution "yesterday."

However, it is important to take into account the schedule for delivering your recommended solution. If decision-makers consider a given solution to be too long for delivery, then it is not feasible. You may still want to press for a given solution if you believe in it, and we will address that with the section on overcoming objections.

TIP

Features are useful mainly to the extent they support the benefits of a recommendation.

Focus on Benefits; Avoid the Feature Fallacy. A common mistake when proposing recommendations or building a business case is to focus on features. The functionality of what a product can do and the features of what it has are always easier to articulate. For Speedy Mortgage, it may be the ability to accept online mortgages. For a retailer, it may be the ability to accept credit card transactions remotely using a smart phone. For our company, a new training registration system offers complete training history for a student in one place.

However compelling the features might seem, they are far less important than the benefits to the business. Features are useful mainly to the extent they support the benefits of a recommendation. For example, an online mortgage capability translates into increased revenues because of quicker application processing and easier access for mortgage applicants. History for a training system means higher sales due to better information on student backgrounds and projected future needs.

To be most influential, we suggest you think of "features and benefits" just like marketers do when promoting their products.

Align Recommendations with the business goals, pain, or opportunities. We think this should be obvious, but it is surprising how many projects get launched without such alignment. The entire SARIE process helps keep recommendations aligned with agreed-on business problems and opportunities. Your recommendations will be more successful if you also keep them aligned with business goals. For example, Speedy Mortgage might have a goal or objective of increasing mortgage revenue by 10% in the coming year, so management will be receptive to a recommendation that will reduce abandoned mortgages.

DOWNLOADABLE TEMPLATE

Rank-order and structure your recommendations. A practical method for focusing on benefits and aligning recommendations is to rank-order or structure them. Here is a tool we have found valuable for doing just that—the Weighted Ranking Matrix.

Weighted Ranking Matrix

A weighted ranking matrix is a useful tool to help us make objective recommendations (and for decision-makers to make rational, objective decisions). In our everyday lives, we make numerous decisions quickly and subconsciously. We use rankings that we aren't even aware of, such as deciding on clothes to buy, picking books to read, or choosing a vacation.

When people are faced with multiple alternatives, the weighted ranking approach can help, especially when the stakes are high. In other words, you wouldn't use this method for proposing which movie you and your spouse should attend this weekend, but it is completely appropriate when using your consulting skills to influence positive outcomes.

Weighted ranking combines pair-matching with weighted criteria to help objectify a decision or recommendation. It is also useful to confirm an initial or intuitive choice.

Constructing a Weighted Ranking Table

Here are the basic steps to create a weighted ranking table, adapted from a practical and valuable book on analytical thinking tools by Morgan Jones, an ex-CIA officer.[6] The example is one we used in our company to purchase an office copier. It helped us make a good choice (and it was not the initial favorite either).

1. List all the major criteria for ranking and **pair-rank the criteria**. Pair-ranking (sometimes called pair-compare ranking) involves matching all the alternatives, two at a time, and voting on which of the two is better or more desirable. See *Figure 23* for an example. The tick marks keep track of votes as you record them.

Items to be Ranked	Times Won in Pairing	Votes
Monthly Payment	| | | |	4
Reliability	| | | | |	5
Number of Source Trays	| |	2
Speed	| | |	3
Footprint		0
Delivery Date	|	1

FIGURE 23: Example Criteria List for Ranking

2. **Construct a weighted-ranking matrix**. Put your list of items to be ranked along the left as rows of your table. Select the top three to seven criteria from your earlier criteria list as columns and weigh those using percentages of importance (totaling 1.0). The criteria and their weights should be the criteria that decision-makers will use to decide on your recommendation. Using criteria in this way applies whether it is a stand-alone decision or one of many competing business cases.

For our copier example, the reliability factor was extremely important since our previous copier was non-functional too much of the time. We needed one that would be highly reliable. Cost and speed were also important to us. See *Figure 24.*

> **TIP**
>
> The criteria and their weights in your table should be the criteria that decision-makers will use to decide on your recommendation.

Items to be Ranked	Criteria (Weight)			Total Votes	Final Ranking
	Reliability Weight: .5	Monthly Payment Weight: .3	Speed Weight: .2		
Canon					
Kyocera					
Toshiba					
Sharp					

FIGURE 24: Example Weighted-Ranking Matrix

3. **Pair-rank each item** against the others **for each criterion** and record the votes each item receives. In this example, there are six compares for each criterion: Canon vs. Kyocera, Canon vs. Toshiba, and Canon vs. Sharp, then Kyocera vs. Toshiba, and Kyocera vs. Sharp, finally Toshiba vs. Sharp. (For any such matrix, you can quickly calculate the number of pairings with this formula: $n * (n - 1) / 2$, where n is the number of items to be compared. For our example, the formula yields 4 * (4-1) / 2 or 6.)

Alternatives to handle the rankings include:

a. Start with the first criterion, such as reliability, for example, and determine with stakeholders whether Canon or Kyocera, Canon or Toshiba, or Canon or Sharp is more reliable. Then, compare Kyocera vs. Toshiba, and Kyocera vs. Sharp. Finally, compare Toshiba vs. Sharp.

b. For each comparison, record which of the pairings got the vote. A simple way to handle this is with a majority rules vote, and it is quick and easy to record the vote for which pair won.

c. A more complicated and nuanced alternative is to record how many stakeholders vote for each pairing, meaning you will record one vote per person for the item judged better for the particular criterion. If five people vote, you might record three votes for Canon and two for Kyocera, for example.

d. Yet another alternative that acknowledges political realities is to give stakeholders with more authority extra votes and record correspondingly. For example, a department manager might get two votes, and the staff members in that department get one vote.

e. After finishing one criterion, move on to the next and pair-compare all the items and record the votes using tick marks in the matrix as shown in *Figure 25*.

	Criteria (Weight)			Total Votes	Final Ranking
Items to be Ranked	**Reliability** Weight: .5	**Monthly Payment** Weight: .3	**Speed** Weight: .2		
Canon	I I I	I I	I I		
Kyocera	I	I	I		
Toshiba		I I I			
Sharp	I I		I I I		

FIGURE 25: Example Pair-Rankings

4. Multiply the votes by each criterion's weight to get a weighted score. Do this for each of the votes recorded for each of the criteria for each item. The maximum calculations in the above example will be 12 (4 items * 3 criteria), but because two of the items got no votes on some criteria, there are only nine calculations. See *Figure 26* for an example.

5. Add the weighted votes for each item and total the sum in the column "Total Votes."

6. Record final rankings in the column marked "Final Ranking." If you are making a recommendation for a specific copier, software package, candidate to be hired, etc., this ranking becomes the order of preference. The item ranked second becomes an alternative if the first ranked item is not acceptable for whatever reason.

7. Perform a "sanity check" to make sure the results make sense to the participants. If an item scores extremely high or low, it might indicate the results are skewed. While surprises are common and uncovering surprises is a side benefit to doing this process, unrealistic results are not helpful. Weighted rankings are meant to increase stakeholder confidence in the final recommendation or decision. If we don't trust the outcome, it usually means we need to refine the criteria and/or strive for more objective ways to compare the items.

Items to be Ranked	Criteria (Weight)			Total Votes	Final Ranking
	Reliability Weight: .5	Monthly Payment Weight: .3	Speed Weight: .2		
Canon	3*.5 = 1.5	2*.3 = .6	2*.2 = .4	2.5	1
Kyocera	1*.5 = .5	1*.3 = .3	1*.2 = .2	1.0	3
Toshiba		3*.3 = .9		0.9	4
Sharp	2 *.5=1.0		3*.2 = .6	1.6	2

FIGURE 26: Example Weighted-Ranking Table With Votes and Results

Recommendation Example

Remember the Speedy Mortgage problem? The recommendation for them might look like this:

Improve the mortgage application and verification processes first before implementing any software package. Perform "as-is" and "to-be" process mapping, and analyze the gaps. Use the process map to search for a mortgage processing package.

Implementation

A recommendation without a plan to carry it out is just a good idea. We all have plenty of those, but a trusted advisor will also present an implementation approach along with a recommendation to make it reality. That is what the "I" in SARIE reminds us to include, namely an implementation outline.

The implementation step is not a project plan or even a project charter. After all, the proposal may not be approved, and any detailed planning would be a waste if the recommendation is not approved. Instead, here are some of the main points to include in the "I" part of SARIE:

- How will the recommendation be implemented?
- What will it cost? How difficult is it to produce? Do we have the needed resources to implement the proposal?
- What is the approach? A software package? A custom solution? Outsourcing?

- Who will be affected by the change?

There are two tools we have found helpful in planning the implementation of a recommendation: the Selection matrix and RACI matrix. Let's examine them to see how they can help in the "I" stage.

a) Selection Matrix (also called a Pay-Off Matrix)

A selection matrix (or pay-off matrix) is a useful tool to help guide implementation because it structures recommendations according to how beneficial they are and how easy they are to implement. The matrix as we use it has two main variables:

- The benefit of a proposed solution or its parts, from low to high.
- The difficulty of implementing a proposed solution, from easy to hard.

By dividing the matrix into four quadrants, it is easier to categorize the parts of our recommendation, especially to show which parts have the most influence. The categories guide both the selection of the components and their implementation. See *Figure 27* for the four categories, briefly described below and in our downloadable template.

DOWNLOADABLE TEMPLATE

- **Prioritize** – high benefit, difficult/time-consuming to implement
- **Quick Hit** – high benefit, easy to implement
- **Wish List** – low benefit, easy to implement
- **Toss** – low benefit, difficult to implement

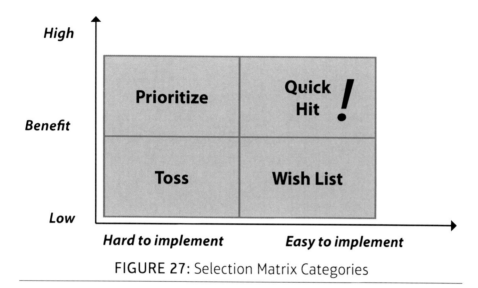

FIGURE 27: Selection Matrix Categories

For example, let us re-visit Speedy Mortgage. Suppose the overall recommendation for our SARIE is a new system and processes for handling mortgage production. The matrix could be constructed as follows:

- **Prioritize**. A website that accepts mortgage applications and improved quality and speed are beneficial but will take time and resources to create. They are placed in the "Prioritize" quadrant for high benefit-hard to produce. Prioritize means that further breakdown of the benefits of and costs associated with implementing is needed. See *Figure 28.*

- **Quick Hit**. A deliverable, such as a standard application form to be used by all sales offices and a new process to do mortgage verifications simultaneously instead of sequentially, would be beneficial and could be relatively easy to do. (The new form is easier, so it is placed father to the right.) These so-called "quick hits," or "low hanging fruit" as some would say, are the places to start implementing, unless there are dependencies forcing a different starting place.

- **Wish List**. Some proposals might have lower perceived value to the organization, for example, emailing credit bureau reports to borrowers. Because these may also be easy, it may be tempting to work on them before other parts of a solution. However, the "Wish List" items divert resources from the harder to accomplish but higher value "Prioritize" items. Our advice it to use them as filler projects and to work on them after the higher-benefit components are completed.

- **Toss**. If a proposal or one of its portions is of low benefit and hard to produce, like the data feed in the example, one might ask, "Why bother?" Yet, how many projects do we work on that seem to have components that would fit in this quadrant? (Richard had a student who once commented, "Gee, the Toss category explains a lot of my projects!" He was only half joking.) By placing a recommendation into the low benefit/hard-to-produce category, we can easily see there is little pay-off. And, that will in turn help decision-makers make the decision to "toss" the recommendation.

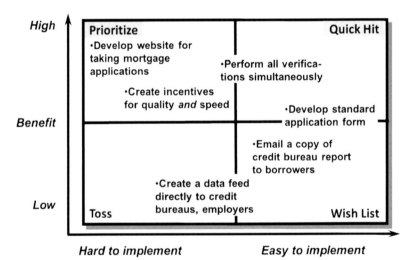

FIGURE 28: Example Selection Matrix

Challenges

The main challenge with a Selection matrix is to objectively determine the benefit and difficulty. If your recommendation (or portions of it) has tangible benefits, you can more easily rate them on the benefit scale. If you have detailed time-and-cost estimates for producing the deliverables in your proposal, it also eases the placement on the difficulty scale.

However, what if your recommendation only has intangible benefits? What if the difficulty can only be guessed at by the people who will produce them? Both the benefits and difficulty assessments can be highly subjective, and their accuracy will depend on how well you can facilitate stakeholder consensus judgment. The matrix becomes a way to document the benefit and difficulty decisions made by stakeholders. As such, its visual nature is an excellent reminder for what to focus on—namely, the high-benefit items.

It is beyond the scope of this book to delve into cost-benefit analysis or even how to estimate tangible benefits. A book we have found valuable for describing benefit identification as part of creating business cases is *Making Technology Investments Profitable: ROI Road Map from Business Case to Value Realization* by Jack Keen.[6]

Traceability

A method commonly used in managing requirements for IT projects is traceability. When managing requirements, traceability helps ensure that requirements link back to and support project deliverables, project objectives, business problems, and/or business objectives. It is used to help prevent rogue requirements from sneaking into a project.

The same link-back approach can help analyze how well a solution component supports business objectives or solves business problems. The more a recommendation does this, the higher benefit level it has in a selection matrix.

> **TIP**
>
> Use the concept of traceability to help structure your recommendations on the benefit scale. Analyzing how well each component helps solve business problems and reach objectives will assist you in placing them into a selection matrix.

To summarize, a Selection matrix is a highly visual and organized way to represent proposed solution portions along two crucial variables: benefit and difficulty. It will facilitate the selection of your solution or its components by decision-makers and guide their implementation. By showing a practical path to carry out a proposal, it is easier to influence others to accept your recommendation.

b) RACI Matrix

RACI matrices are valuable tools to help with the implementation of a recommendation. They are described as part of stakeholder analysis in Chapter 5, so this section will focus on how to use RACI to help with implementation.

As a review, RACI stands for who is **R**esponsible for something, who is **A**ccountable, who to **C**onsult with, and who to **I**nform. These four categories, along with an optional Support category, identify the crucial roles for getting things done. See *Table 17* for an example of applying RACI to the implementation stage of SARIE.

- **R:** The person assigned to the R is responsible for accomplishing what you recommend. Often, this is a project manager or business analyst, and it can be left blank if no person has been assigned yet.

- **A:** The A person approves the deliverable and accepts it as done. We often view this as the sponsor role. The Accountable role is one source of the potential benefits of a solution and is important to include when assessing the benefits scale for a selection matrix.

- **C:** The C people provide their advice and input to the team producing the deliverable. We often view this role as subject matter experts (SMEs), which could be part of the domain in question (i.e., the business area in which the change is occurring). Domain SMEs can help articulate and judge the benefits of a recommendation. Or the people you list in the C category may be "implementation SMEs" whose input is needed to plan and implement the approach. They are important sources for determining the difficulty scale for a proposed solution component.

- **I:** The I role in RACI is a list of who to inform that a change is being planned and implemented. It usually contains people directly affected by a change but can include those indirectly affected, including external customers of the organization.

Proposal	R	A	C	I
Develop Standard Application	Project Manager	Sponsor	Sr. Mortgage Sales	Mortgage Sales, Verification Dept.
Change verification Process	Project Manager	Sponsor	Verification Leads	Verification Dept., Mortgage Sales
Develop Web Site for Mortgage Apps	Project Manager	Sponsor	All affected Group	Entire company
Create New Incentives	Project Manager	Sponsor	HR, Sr. Mortgage Sales	Mortgage Sales

TABLE 17: Example RACI for Guiding Implementation

To recap, a RACI matrix is a useful tool to capture the important roles for a change initiative. It helps manage change and build credibility and trust because of the input you elicit and by informing

TIP

The "A" people in RACI are important to include when assessing the benefits scale for a selection matrix.

The "C" people from RACI will help you determine the difficulty scale in the selection matrix.

people affected by a change. It is one of our favorite tools for influencing positive outcomes.

Evaluation

The evaluation stage of the SARIE process has two purposes:

1. **Pre-Implementation**. To develop metrics for how the recommended solution (project) will be evaluated. *Table 18* provides examples of metrics that can be used for evaluations.

How much will direct revenue be increased as a result of new capabilities?
How many new customers will be obtained?
How much will market share improve as a result?
How much cost-savings will result from the recommendation?
How much "cycle time" for an improved process will be saved?
How much time will be saved in producing key outputs?
Will the number of unneeded inputs and outputs in a process be reduced?
How much cost savings will there be in producing outputs of a process?
How much will rework be reduced (waste, scrap, defects) and what will it save?
What is the time/cost of required approvals? What can we save by reducing or automating them, assuming there is little added risk?

How much will employee morale improve? How do we measure it? What is the cost of not improving morale?

TABLE 18: Evaluation Metrics Samples

2. **Post-Implementation**. This second use of the "E" in SARIE addresses how effective the recommended change will be in solving the business problem or seizing the opportunity identified in the "S" stage of the process. It is helpful to us as trusted advisors to know whether or not our recommendation did indeed help the organization achieve its goals. This is sometimes called an "outcomes assessment" in healthcare and education.

> **TIP**
>
> Be sure to include any evaluation measurements and a mechanism to capture and report them in the new capabilities you introduce.

The evaluation stage of the SARIE process is optional, but important. Over time, we learned the value of evaluating a recommendation. As business owners ourselves, we have had our share of painful lessons learned by implementing what sounded like good ideas but turned out to not be as effective or that cost more than we anticipated. Now we suggest treating the evaluation step as a required one to properly complete the consulting cycle. Think of it as an important punctuation to any recommendation.

Challenges in Performing Evaluations

There are significant challenges with evaluating recommendations and their subsequent performance. One tricky issue is in determining who or what is responsible for the change. We recommend solutions and ways to implement those solutions. However, even if our recommendations are accepted, they may be implemented haphazardly or with little consideration for the readiness of those affected stakeholders.

As an example, let's say you recommended a new training program for employees in a high-turnover job. If you conduct an evaluation and discover the productivity of the workers in that job increased, you may want to

> **TIP**
>
> Be careful that you do not own the decision to implement your recommendation. We advise; the sponsor decides. However, we do need feedback on how well our recommendations helped the organization.

conclude that your recommendation succeeded and led to the increase. But, as stated in an earlier example, if the company also hired a higher caliber of employee and increased their pay, then to what extent did those changes contribute to the project's success?

What seems relevant to point out in a book on influencing is this warning: if you accept credit for your recommendations that succeed, then be prepared to accept blame for the ones that fail, too.

We think that if you can foster agreement or consensus on which measurement items to include in your evaluation, then you have achieved a significant step.

The next step is to then measure those items after the recommendation is implemented. The "E" part of SARIE will help you get there. Of course, be sure to include those measurements and a mechanism to capture and report them in the new capabilities you introduce.

Consulting Summary

Consulting can assist your influence in the following ways:

- It is a highly logical and rational process, which many decision-makers prefer. It is perhaps the best way to remove possible hidden agendas behind recommendations.
- It excels by fostering an agreement on the situation before trying to explain it or, worse yet, "jumping to a solution." By first defining the business problem or opportunity, then getting to the root causes or main drivers, the most sensible or rational solution may become obvious.
- Consulting is a highly learnable skill that is effective in nearly every environment.

There are some possible disadvantages to consulting:

- For small efforts, the entire SARIE process may seem like overkill to people. We suggest keeping it simple on small consulting efforts, and consider doing a SARIE by email. Yes, seriously. We request that frequently in our own company when staff members want to influence us.

> **TIP**
>
> As you learn the consulting method, start by discovering the business situation at hand, and keep reminding people of it as your work progresses into a project.

- On a related note, it does take time to complete the full SARIE cycle to achieve the benefits of it. A possible shortcut in time-constrained environments is to complete at least a "SAR," or the first three parts of SARIE. That way, if the recommendation stands a chance of being adopted, you can later complete the "I" and "E" portions.

- If done too rationally, consulting may underestimate and even ignore some of the emotional aspects of influencing. The analytical consulting tools may not always address stakeholder feelings and attitudes, and as internal consultants, we should be watching for these factors in addition to evidence and facts.

Our Advice:

- Use the SARIE model to guide your consulting. By doing so, you can achieve more influence with stakeholders, particularly management.

- As you learn it, focus on one step at a time. Start by discovering the business situation at hand, and keep reminding people of it as your work progresses into a project.

- Use the various analysis tools that are appropriate to the situation. Not all the tools work well or are needed in every circumstance.

Summary

- We cannot overemphasize the importance of consulting and advising when working to become more influential. Unless we have positional or reward power, we must use our personal and expert power to influence others.

- A consultative approach is the best way we've found to reach the trusted advisor role. That role in turn leads to the influence that those of us without authority want to achieve.

- The consulting method of preparation we presented here is the SARIE approach to consulting. SARIE is a practical and repeatable approach with five major components:

  S – Situation: *Understanding the business need*

  A – Analysis: *Analyzing the business need (ask questions, determine impacts, and alternatives)*

  R – Recommendation: *Recommending a course of action*

  I – Implementation: *Providing guidance on how to implement the recommendations*

  E – Evaluation: *Helping to evaluate if the business need was satisfied*

- We discussed many tools in this chapter to help with a consulting effort. Different problems and opportunities require different tools, and you may inherently prefer some over the others. (We have our own favorites.) To help you recall and apply the right tool for the right situation, *Table 19* provides a summary and some guidance.

- The technique of consultative questioning is essential to the consultation/advising role. The next chapter explores that topic in depth.

Summary of Consulting Tools			
Tool	**Description**	**Example**	**Tips for Usage**
Situation Statement	Defines the business problem or opportunity that needs to be addressed	Mortgage applications at Speedy Mortgage require on average 45 days to process compared to the previous average of 30 days and the industry benchmark of 32. The slower processing delays mortgage approvals and final closing at an estimated cost of $100 per closed loan. Delays also cause 5% of loans to be abandoned, losing $10,000 revenue per loan, or $1.2 million per year.	Seek to understand and document the situation before attempting to explain or solve it. Good question to ask: "What business problem are we trying to solve?"
Five Whys	Ask "why" diplomatically up to five times to understand the root cause.	N/A	Determine appropriate ways of asking "why" that don't irritate your stakeholders. Examples: "Help me understand…" "What did you try previously, and why didn't it work?" "What has limited you in today's environment and why?"

Summary of Consulting Tools

Tool	Description	Example	Tips for Usage
Mind Maps	A visual cause-and-effect diagram that uses a problem at the center and branches into causes and sub-causes		Mind maps help to: • Probe deeper and deeper. • Facilitate recording relevant factors. • Coherently record ideas. • Keep brainstorming. Use along with Five Whys, but more than two or three levels deep gets overly crowded.

Summary of Consulting Tools

Tool	Description	Example	Tips for Usage
Fishbone Diagrams	Another visual cause-and-effect diagram, much like a Mind map, that uses standard groups as cause categories	*(Fishbone diagram: Customer reports not getting out on time; categories include Equipment [Operating System, Win98], Materials [Insufficient Paper, Shortage of Data Entry Staff], Methods [Database Extract Delays, Scheduling], People [Low Wages])*	Production Categories: Policy, Procedure, Place, Customer, Systems Service Categories: Equipment, Methods, Materials, Measurements, Environment Use along with Five Whys, but more than two or three levels deep gets overly crowded.
Process Diagrams	Process maps that also help us to look for causes of process problems and gaps in capabilities, including missing capabilities	*(Process diagram: Assemble Product → Deliver Product to Shipping → Queue Shipments → Deliver Shipments to Shipper → Delayed Shipments)*	For each step in a process, ask, "How might this step contribute to the problem?" Resist temptation to improve the process before finding the root cause of a problem first.

Summary of Consulting Tools

Tool	Description	Example	Tips for Usage
Inter-relationship Diagrams	Special kind of cause-and-effect diagram that looks at the causes uncovered by fishbone diagrams and mind maps, and inter-relates them. Look for the causes that create the most effects, and fix those first.	**PROBLEM:** Customer reports are not getting out on time	Compare causes and effects to see which ones are related. Look for the causes which create the most effects; those are the ones to fix first.

Summary of Consulting Tools

Tool	Description	Example	Tips for Usage
Pareto Diagrams	Diagrams that utilize the 80/20 rule and show the most significant contributors to a problem, ordered by their frequency from highest to lowest		Aim is to find 20% of the factors that cause 80% of the problem. Needs a problem that can be measured and categorized into variables.
Scatter Diagrams	Diagrams that show trends and correlations between two sets of variables.		The straighter the line with the diagram, the stronger the case for correlation.

Summary of Consulting Tools

Tool	Description	Example	Tips for Usage
Feasibility Analysis	A technique for determining the feasibility of your recommendation	N/A	Use the TELOS framework: • Technology. • Economic. • Legal. • Operational. • Schedule.
Weighted Ranking Matrix	Uses a small set of important criteria, weighted to decision-makers' priorities, to help make objective decisions given limited number of choices	*(see matrix below)*	Use pair-ranking to first rank the criteria. Formula for how many pair-compares to do: $n * (n - 1) / 2$. Apply a "sanity check" to results.

Items to be Ranked	Criteria (Weight)			Total Votes	Final Ranking
	Reliability Weight: .5	Monthly Payment Weight: .3	Speed Weight: .2		
Canon	3*.5=1.5	2*.3=.6	2*.2=.4	2.5	1
Kyocera	1*.5=.5	1*.3=.3	1*.2=.2	1.0	3
Toshiba		3*.3=.9		0.9	4
Sharp	2*.5=1.0		3*.2=.6	1.6	2

Summary of Consulting Tools

Tool	Description	Example	Tips for Usage
Selection Matrix (also known as a Pay-Off Matrix)	Helps guide implementation by structuring recommendations by how beneficial they are and how easy they are to implement	Benefit (High to Low) vs. Hard to implement / Easy to implement. Quadrants: Prioritize, Quick Hit, Toss, Wish List	Focus on Quick Hits and Prioritize: • Quick Hit: high benefit, easy to implement. • Prioritize: high benefit, difficult or time-consuming to implement. • Wish List: low benefit, easy to implement. • Toss: low benefit, difficult to implement.

Summary of Consulting Tools			
Tool	**Description**	**Example**	**Tips for Usage**
RACI Diagrams	Role and responsibility matrix, indicating who is Responsible for something, who is Accountable, who to Consult with, and who to Inform.	<table><tr><td>Proposal</td><td>R</td><td>A</td><td>C</td><td>I</td></tr><tr><td>Develop Standard Application</td><td>Project Manager</td><td>Sponsor</td><td>Sr. Mortgage Sales</td><td>Mortgage Sales, Verification Dept.</td></tr><tr><td>Change verification Process</td><td>Project Manager</td><td>Sponsor</td><td>Verification Leads</td><td>Verification Dept., Mortgage Sales</td></tr><tr><td>Develop Web Site for Mortgage Apps</td><td>Project Manager</td><td>Sponsor</td><td>All affected Group</td><td>Entire company</td></tr><tr><td>Create New Incentives</td><td>Project Manager</td><td>Sponsor</td><td>HR, Sr. Mortgage Sales</td><td>Mortgage Sales</td></tr></table>	• When used with consulting, can influence selection of a recommendation through well-planned responsibilities.

TABLE 19: Consulting Tools Summary

1   Edward de Bono. "Creativity Quotes," Innovation Tools, accessed March 02, 2012, http://www.innovationtools.com/Quotes/QuotesDetail.asp?CatID=2 .

2   Malcolm Craig. Thinking Visually: Business Applications of 14 Core Diagrams (London, England: Thomson Learning, 2000), 39.

3   Gladewell.com. accessed May 09, 2012, http://www.gladwell.com/2011/2011_05_16_a_creationmyth.html.

4   Vijay Govindarajan and Jay Terwilliger. "Yes, You Can Brainstorm Without Groupthink", HBR Blog Network, accessed August 02, 2012, http://blogs.hbr.org/cs/2012/07/yes_you_can_brainstorm_without.html

5   TELOS (project management), Wikipedia: The Free Encyclopedia, accessed May 14, 2011, http://en.wikipedia.org/wiki/TELOS_(project_management).

6   Morgan D. Jones. The Thinker's Toolkit: 14 Powerful Techniques for Problem Solving (New York, NY: Three Rivers Press, 1998).

7   Jack Keen. Making Technology Investments Profitable: ROI Road Map from Business Case to Value Realization, 2nd ed. (Hoboken, NJ: Wiley, 2011).

07 Consultative Questioning

> *"You can tell whether people are clever by their answers. You can tell whether they are wise by their questions."*
>
> **NAGUIB MAHFOUZ**
> NOBEL PRIZE AUTHOR

An important aspect to influencing is to prepare and ask consultative questions. It involves a collaborative style of questioning, which together with the client's input helps discover their needs and wants. Such questioning helps ensure commitment to projects and other initiatives and increases buy-in for your resulting recommendations.

What we mean by consultative questioning is questioning that has one or more of these attributes:

- Is professional and respectful and does not use leading questions.
- Builds credibility, trust, and buy-in.
- Is incisive and helps get to the root cause of a problem.
- Requires planning and research to prepare good questions.
- Uses effective listening skills while asking questions, especially to paraphrase and pursue unforeseen issues and concerns.
- Often involves follow-up questions or future research to get complete information.
- Discovers how stakeholders feel about an issue, particularly their attitude towards change.
- Leads to good advice, recommendations, and alternatives for clients.

Background

To be most effective, consultative questioning treats each formal session like any other meeting or requirements elicitation session. When planning the session and inviting participants, make sure you know the reason for the session and what you hope to accomplish. Too often we hurry into an interview or start asking questions without understanding these two things.

There are two essential ingredients to any effective meeting, and consultative questioning is no different. What you should always identify are:

1. The reason why the session is needed (Objective);
2. What you hope to walk away with (the Desired Outcome).

These two elements will help you plan what you want from the session and will guide the questions you prepare. They will alert participants to the session scope and what you want to accomplish. You can use the two ingredients to help you facilitate the session, especially to keep people from drifting into unproductive side-tangents.

TIP

Two key items to prepare before any consultative questioning session are:

1. What is the objective

2. What is the desired outcome

These are helpful in any meeting context, and we use them religiously in our company and client meetings. Our staff occasionally grumble when putting them together, but the objectives and desired outcome are hugely beneficial for contributing to productive meetings in our company.

Take a look at two examples, stated from the perspective of a project manager and a business analyst.

Example 1: *"We're close to exceeding the project budget. I need to find out if my project will get extra funding…or not. What I need is a decision from the sponsor on whether we can get more funding or if the project will be put on hold."*

Objective: Determine status of funding for the project

Desired Outcome: Decision on additional funding or whether to put the project on hold

Example 2: *"I need to understand the high-level requirements for this project before we go any further. I need to find out all the desired features and functions in scope for the new project."*

Objective: Define the high-level requirements for this project

Desired Outcome: An approved list of high-level requirements for this project

Active Listening

An important element for consultative questioning is the ability to listen actively and effectively. There are many books and resources on listening, so we won't be exhaustive or detailed here. Consult any of the other resources on the subject.

Instead, we want to reinforce some good habits and remind you of a couple of key points about listening.

- *Listen Actively* – To understand the answers you hear, listen actively. Some helpful phrases to use that will help with active listening are:
  - Tell me more about…
  - Let me see if I can summarize…
  - What I heard you say is…
  - Let me see if I understand…
  - Could you elaborate on…
  - How do you feel/what do you think about…

- *Watch Non-Verbals* – Only 7% of the effect of any communication is verbal. Research shows 38% comes from the tone of voice used by the speaker and 55% comes from facial gestures and expressions.[1]

- *Be Respectful of the Speaker* – Don't interrupt. Limit distractions. Don't answer your cell phone. In short, be "present."

- *Paraphrase* – This is the difficult art of listening to what is said and re-stating in different words. It requires absolute focus and the ability to synthesize the information you're hearing, decide what's important, and repeat back what you heard using different words. Effective paraphrasing is an advanced skill. Summarizing works well as an alternative.

- *Summarize* – Save time at the end of every session to summarize key decisions and action items.

- *Take Notes* – This shows respect and helps you to recall the conversation. Share your notes with the interviewee and have them correct any misunderstandings.

Effective Questioning – E.G.O. Framework

A useful acronym to help you structure any interview situation, not just consultative questioning, is called the E.G.O. approach. Use it to help structure your consultative and other questions. It stands for:

E – Environment. Establish rapport, and work on generating trust with your client. It also deals with the organization environment and finding out where your client fits in it.

EGO FRAMEWORK

Helps structure interview questions:

E – Environment. Learn about the organization and client.

G – Goals. Learn what your client would like to accomplish.

O – Obstacles. Consider what may prevent goals being met.

G – Goals. Determine the goals your client would like to accomplish within their organizational area. For instance, your client may need to speed up the times for processing drivers' licenses. Or they may need to increase the quality of products being built.

O – Obstacles. Identify the current obstacles to overcoming their goals. An example of an obstacle might be that the drivers' license process is mostly manual and time intensive. Another example of an obstacle might be that the parts procurement process is outdated and inefficient.

The gap between goals and obstacles provides opportunities for consultants to add value and exert influence. By focusing on the gaps, we can best leverage our time to provide the most benefit from any recommended solution. It also helps us avoid jumping to solutions, particularly when combined with the root cause analysis, described earlier.

> **TIP**
>
> The gap between goals and obstacles provides opportunities for trusted advisors to add value and exert influence.

Logical vs. Emotional Questions

We are more likely to understand what a person thinks by finding out how they feel. We can't rely *solely* on emotion, though, because emotions change and therefore requirements or priorities may change when that happens.

One of the best ways to get insights quickly is to focus on the type of language a person uses. The noted sales authority Zig Ziglar describes ways in which sales professionals use effective questioning to understand buyers' needs.

Ziglar refers to Neuro-Linguistic Programming (NLP) to categorize high-level communication styles.[2]

NLP is described in Chapter 5, Stakeholder Analysis. As a quick review, Neuro-Linguistic Programming defines three types of ways in which we perceive the world. We tend to favor one or two primary types and use them consistently. Our questions for them should be framed in the same language.

1. *Visual language* leads people to respond logically (e.g., think of the phrase "seeing is believing"). Visual communicators use expressions such as "I can see the problem" or "How does it look to you?" They love visual charts, graphs, and summaries and need to see a document or explanation to truly understand it. Stakeholders with this style will make decisions based on logic.

2. *Auditory language* leads to emotional involvement (e.g., "you can't believe everything you hear"). People who prefer auditory communication will use expressions such as "I hear you!" or "Sounds good" or "How does that sound?" Auditory perceivers can listen and readily understand words without the benefit of visuals or pictures. They tend to hate lengthy documents and PowerPoint presentations.

3. *Kinesthetic language* leads to empathy and ownership (e.g., the expression "I wanted it so badly I could taste it."). Kinesthetic or tactile communicators will use expressions such as "I can get my arms around that" or "Where does the matter stand?" These type of perceivers need to get their hands on something, whether it be a prototype or at a white board or a computer keyboard.

If you are having trouble connecting with the people you are trying to influence, try matching your language style with that of the other person.

A favorite example of ours is that of a business analyst whom we'll call Carol, who works at a major client of ours, a Fortune 100 retailer. She was working on a high-profile project and giving an important summary of her requirements to the executive team, including the CIO, Peter. Being a visual type of perceiver, Carol spent hours working on a PowerPoint presentation and labored on the visual summaries of her findings. It was a "thing of beauty" she told us, and she spent time rehearsing and revising the slide deck to get it just right.

Well, the big day arrived, and the presentation began. Carol got past her nervousness, and with heads nodding, she thought it was going well. That is, until Peter closed his eyes about a quarter of the way into the presentation. Carol kept going but thought she had completely blown the presentation and the project. Peter kept his eyes closed until Carol said, "Well, that wraps it up," and Peter suddenly opened his eyes again. Carol could barely look at him because she was so embarrassed. Then, she was flabbergasted when he said "Great job, I'd like to move forward. What about the rest of you?"

She later realized (in class when she heard about the three types of perceivers) that Peter was primarily an auditory perceiver, and she approached him as if he were a visual perceiver. People later told her that Peter *always* closes his eyes during a presentation, and that she need not have worried. The lesson learned from this example is to discover the communication preferences of your audience and then present information and ask questions in a way that engages that style.

Questions to Understand the "Why"

As discussed in the section on analyzing root causes of problems in Chapter 6, as consultants we need to thoroughly understand why a given situation exists. Yet, merely asking the question "why" can be irritating to clients. (If, like us, you have raised children and experienced a child's constant chorus of "why?" to understand the world, then you know how irritating it can be. Our eight-year-old grandson has perfected this art and has made a game of it. For example, he might ask "Do you like salad?" When we answer "yes," he'll ask "Why?" Then, "What's your favorite vegetable?" When we answer "tomatoes," he'll ask "Why do you like tomatoes?" and so it goes until we stop playing—which is very soon)

The set of questions below and others like them can help you to ask "why" politely and professionally. Add them to your repertoire to increase your ability to learn why problems exist without irritating your stakeholders. Remember, to go five levels deep in root cause analysis, you need a variety of ways of asking "why" to get to the root cause.

TIP

To go five levels deep in root cause analysis, you need a variety of ways of asking "why" to get to the root cause.

"Help me understand _____"

"What causes _____?"

"What is the business need for _____?"

"What are you trying to accomplish with _____?"

"What business problem are we trying to solve?"

The latter might be our favorite. It has helped both of us on numerous occasions to focus a conversation on a business problem and to help avoid jumping to solutions.

Categories of Questions to Get Started

To ensure a complete set of questions about an issue, it is often helpful to frame them in a set of typical categories. For requirements analysis on IT projects, we have written about the categories of Process, Data, Interaction, and Interface. One of our articles in particular covers this topic in some depth and is included as Appendix A: "101+ of the Most Effective Questions You Can Ask to Elicit Requirements and Uncover Expectations."

TIP

This article is also available along with many others on our website at: www.watermarklearning.com/articles.php.

For generic situations, the following categories are usually sufficient to get started planning your consultative questions. Use this list as a beginning point and develop more detailed questions to fit the particular problem or opportunity you are working on. The list is made up of the five "W" questions:

Who/who not?	Who performs this process?
What/what not?	What exceptions are there?
When/when not?	When are inputs not needed?
Where/where not?	Where is the performed?
Why/why not?	Why is the needed?

There is also a non-W question that can be helpful as well:

The Business "How" (vs. technical "How")
How do you determine ?

Questions to Avoid

Avoid leading questions. Questions *motivate* clients to open up and share their needs. Otherwise, leading questions give the impression the questioner has a hidden agenda and is pushing a certain solution. This also helps build trust. Zig Ziglar in his book, *Ziglar on Selling: The Ultimate Handbook for the Complete Sales Professional* cautions against using leading questions during the sales process, and consulting and influencing are no different.[3]

Below is a list of common leading questions we all tend to use. Do you recognize which ones you use most often?

If you catch yourself using these, try rephrasing into a form that will lead to learning or discovery.

"Don't you think that _____?"

"Why don't you _____?"

"Isn't it better to _____?"

"Wouldn't you like to _____?"

"Have you ever thought about a _____?"

"Would you consider_____?"

Example: Instead of asking "Have you ever thought about a website?" one could ask instead "What types of solutions have you tried in the past, and why haven't they worked?" or "What has limited you in today's environment?"

Open-Ended vs. Closed-Ended Questions. Use these two categories of questions appropriately, employing open-ended questions to **uncover needs** and closed-ended questions to **confirm specifics**. Closed-ended questions provide choices and therefore limit the respondents' answers. These questions have the answer embedded in the question (as in a questionnaire) or implied (yes or no). Elizabeth notes some bad advice received early in her career that one should "always use open-ended questions to determine what clients want." That may be fine when beginning a discussion but breaks down when we need to start getting pointed answers.

Here are some basic guidelines we've found useful for asking open- vs. closed-ended questions.

- Open-ended: Use open-ended questions to allow clients to think out loud and to explore their own needs and requirements. The "who, what, when, where, why, and how" questions are usually stated as open-ended.
- Closed-ended: Use closed-ended questions to choose and to confirm. Closed-ended questions are useful when gathering quantitative information (e.g., Of these 20 requirements, which ten are your ten highest priority?). Also, you may need an affirmation or confirmation of something, such as clarifying an assumption (e.g., "This is what I thought I heard you say. Did I get it right?").
- Beware of leading questions because they are usually closed-ended questions that lead to an answer the questioner wants to hear.
- See Appendix A, "101+ of the Most Effective Questions You Can Ask to Elicit Requirements and Uncover Expectations" for a list of useful questions, broken into categories, such as General, Philosophy Toward Requirements, Fundamentals, etc.

Open-Ended Questions

Open-ended questions foster divergent thinking, which is needed to get the perspectives of different stakeholders. Divergent thinking uncovers issues, concerns, and areas that we investigate in order to reach consensus.

Here are some examples of useful open-ended questions to foster divergent-type thinking and uncover expectations as well as needs and requirements:

- What is the business need?
- What are the biggest business problems you face by not having this "widget?" (Substitute a solution or new product for widget.)
- What does "widget" mean to you? Describe your concept and vision.
- How important is this "widget" to you?
- How will you know "it" has been achieved?
- Paired extremes—describe the best widget and why it was the best and repeat for the worst widget.

Closed-Ended Questions

Here are some sample closed-ended questions to foster convergent-type thinking to obtain specific answers and work towards a decision:

- Quantifying:
  - How many "widgets" do you process?
  - How often?
  - When/time of day?
  - Day of week?
- Choice: Would you rather…
- Ranking: What are your priorities?
- Do you use this ___ information?
- Of x, y, or z, which do you prefer?
- Is your trade off time, budget, or scope?

Table 20 is a matrix showing key characteristics of open-ended and closed-ended questions. It was developed and is copyrighted by Anderson, Heidorn & Associates, Inc. and is used with their permission.

	Open-Ended Questions	Closed-Ended Questions
Characteristic	• Unstructured responses • Often describes current state	• Quantitative • Often describes the end state
Types	• Word association • Sentence/paragraph completion • Story completion	• Yes/no • Short answer • Multiple choice • Ranking • Assessment
Advantages	• Greater freedom of expression • No bias due to limited response ranges • Participants can qualify their answers • Can reveal more completely how the participant thinks • Less likely that the participant is pushed or guided to a specific answer	• Can help focus answers • Best for confirmation • Quick to answer • Easy to capture accurate information • No difference between articulate and inarticulate participants

	Open-Ended Questions	Closed-Ended Questions
Disadvantages	• Time-consuming to interpret • Interviewer/facilitator may misinterpret and therefore misclassify a response	• Does not encourage conversation or relationship building • Can draw misleading conclusions because of the limited range of options • Interviewer/facilitator cannot deal with qualifications to responses (particularly in a questionnaire)
When to Use	Need to understand the business reasons and/or process behind the requirement Building relationships Complex information	Narrow choices Confirm Have little time to gather information Need quantitative information Need simplistic information

TABLE 20: Open- and Closed-Ended Questions

Summary

- A key skill in consulting, and therefore in influencing, is consultative questioning.
- As trusted advisors and influencers, we are known by the quality of our questions and the results of our recommendations. The latter is not possible unless you understand the needs and values of the decision-makers you want to influence.

1   Albert Mehrabian and Morton Wiener. Journal of Personality and Social Psychology, Vol 6(1), May 1967, 109-114, accessed December 10, 2011, http://psycnet.apa.org/journals/psp/6/1/109/.

2   Zig Ziglar. *Ziglar on Selling: The Ultimate Handbook for the Complete Sales Professional.* (Nashville, TN: Thomas Nelson, 2007).

3   Ibid.

08

Developing the Courage to Be Influential

"To know what is right and not do it is the worst cowardice."

CONFUCIUS

Years ago a boss told Elizabeth in frustration that she was not a risk-taker, a comment which surprised her.

> "In my mind, I took risks all the time. Wasn't I the one who always made recommendations and presented them to non-receptive superiors?
>
> "Wasn't I the one who initiated new ways of managing projects? Wasn't I the one going to bat for team members, some of whom were not viewed as favorably as I thought they should be?
>
> "I asked for an example, and he said that my projects left little to chance and that I was afraid to implement projects when the end products were defective—a good thing from my perspective. While I took any number of personal risks, I was not about to put our organization at risk. This conversation triggered a great deal of internal thought on different types of risks and the relationship between risk and courage."

Just as several years ago we started hearing the word "trust," we are now hearing the word "courage" a great deal. It's popping up in a variety of contexts, including sports, politics, and business to name a few. According to the Institute for Global Ethics, it's become increasingly mentioned as one of the moral values related to "a caring and civil society." It's listed with other values that commonly surface: "honesty, respect, responsibility, fairness, and compassion—characteristics that have become the litmus test for ethical behavior."[1]

Background

Some of the books previously mentioned have discussions on the topic of courage, including Stephen M.R. Covey's *Speed of Trust* (see Chapter 2), in which he discusses courage as an integral part of integrity.[2]

Maister, Green, and Galford's *The Trusted Advisor* explores courage in the discussion about why it is difficult to be the trusted advisor. One reason the authors cite is "it takes a lot of courage to speak the unspeakable."[3] The previously-mentioned white paper on courage from the Institute on Global Ethics provides insight on a variety of aspects on physical and moral courage.

Definitions

As noted above, there are a variety of different ways to think of courage. Courage is facing physical danger. Courage is also facing moral dilemmas. The Institute for Global Ethics states that "moral courage is something that enables the others [characteristics of ethical behavior] to be effective."[4]

Although Dictionary.com defines courage as "the quality of mind or spirit that enables a person to face difficulty, danger, pain, etc., without fear,"[5] we believe that facing those difficulties despite being afraid is the true sign of courage. As Mark Twain said, "Courage is not the absence of fear. It is acting in spite of it."[6] More to our liking is the Merriam-Webster dictionary definition of courage as "mental or moral strength to venture, persevere, and withstand danger, fear, or difficulty."[7]

Indeed, courage might be "the ability to do things that one finds frightening."[8] Elaine Sternberg, in referring to courage in the business world, says, "Business courage is therefore mainly moral, and is most commonly displayed in a steadfast adherence to the fundamental values of justice, honesty, and fairness."[9]

Novels and Movies

Courage has always been a dominant theme in books and movies. From the most courageous Cowardly Lion in *The Wizard of Oz* to the Gryffindors in the Harry Potter series, protagonists have found themselves unwilling participants in dangerous situations. These situations might involve physical danger where the character's life is threatened. Other situations require facing different kinds of danger needing different kinds of courage, such as moral courage, which is needed when acting with integrity is inconvenient, will not solve a short-term problem, or might not be popular.

TIP

Courage needs to be tempered with a good dose of preparedness, which helps prevent against rashness.

Atticus Finch, in Harper Lee's *To Kill a Mockingbird*, shows the moral courage to confront racism in the American South in the late 1930s. Seen through the eyes of his young daughter, Scout, Finch shows courage throughout the novel: "I wanted you to see what real courage is, instead of getting the idea that courage is a man with a gun in his hand. It's when you know you're licked before you begin, but you begin anyway and see it through no matter what."[10] The book, *The Red Badge of Courage*, a novel about the American Civil War by Stephen Crane, examines overcoming one's fear and cowardice to act courageously.

Courage is sometimes seen as the absence of cowardice. Rushing into dangerous situations might be viewed as brave behavior by some and rash behavior by others. However, the Institute for Global Ethics quotes Aristotle as saying that courage is balanced between cowardice and rashness. Perhaps this applies to not only Stephen Crane's hero but to many project professionals as well. Courage, as we know, needs to be tempered with a good dose of preparedness, which helps prevent against rashness.

The movie *Star Wars* is filled with both courage and rashness. In the first movie, Episode IV, Luke's rush to save Princess Leia is more rash than courageous, but facing his past and his father Darth Vader require real courage, as does Darth Vader's saving his son by killing the Emperor. And Han Solo shows real courage in the fight against the Empire, but only after he overcomes his desire to save his own skin.

Seven Barriers to Courage

Being courageous is far harder than it sounds or seems like it should be. It involves taking risks that can put us in harm's way, physically, psychologically, and/or emotionally. There are some very real barriers to courage.

When we ask our students and clients what gets in the way of acting courageously, we usually hear about barriers that fall into one of three categories.

1. The first has to do with culture—organizational and national culture, as well as culture relating to our personal histories.
2. The second is what we call the fear factor.
3. Both the first and second groups of barriers are more difficult to overcome than the third, which is one of perception and which might or might not stem from or lead to the fear factors. This is the category that relates to feeling that we are not allowed to speak out.

Each of the following seven common reasons why people don't feel courageous falls into one of the three categories. We call them the seven barriers to courage.

1. *Organizational culture.* This barrier happens when the work environment discourages employees from offering their opinions or from disagreeing with those in authority. We find this to be true most frequently in organizations that are more siloed than collaborative, where information tends to be viewed as power to be kept internally, where the organizational structure tends to be hierarchical and where information is uni-directional, flowing downhill. In these types of organizations, it is not uncommon to "shoot" the proverbial messenger, who is anyone communicating bad news, project risks, or recommendations that do not align with the organization's current thinking.

2. *National culture.* There are national cultures that tend to be more hierarchical. Elizabeth once taught a class that had students from several countries. A student from Japan asked if he could take photos of the teams collaborating. He said that in his country the professors tended to stand in the front of the room and lecture. Another student in another class from another country said that it was more common for information to be pushed to students than pulled from them. In these cultures, questioning positional power is harder than one where free expression is valued.

> **Seven Barriers to Courage**
>
> 1. Organizational culture.
> 2. National culture.
> 3. Intimidation.
> 4. Personal background.
> 5. Fear of failure.
> 6. Lack of time.
> 7. "They won't let me".

3. *Intimidation.* There are some organizations where intimidation occurs and is permissible. Fortunately, we have not worked in that type of environment, but we have heard plenty of stories. This intimidation can take many forms, such as aggression or humiliation. We have heard of bosses who threaten subordinates. We have heard of verbal lashing of people who are unprepared or who disagree in meetings. We've even heard of people who are asked to leave after their shortcomings are made an example to all others in the room. Subordinates are bullied, humiliated, and treated to sarcasm and belittling. What is the inducement to being courageous in such an organization!

> **TIP**
>
> We can use our expertise and our leadership skills to influence others without ever being formally empowered by someone else.

4. *Personal background.* If we are raised in an environment where we are not rewarded for creativity and exploration, it is less likely that we are going to readily suggest new ways of doing things at work.

5. *Fear of failure and lack of confidence.* We hear that people wonder if "they" (those in charge) will still like or respect the individual. They are concerned that their ideas won't work or might be considered outlandish, or at the other extreme, too obvious. Robert N. Van Wyk defines "two types of cowards." One, he writes, "allows excessive fears to prevent him from carrying out plans," while the other is "so influenced by fear that he never makes any plans."[11]

6. *Lack of time.* We sometimes hear clients say, "I'm up to my eyeballs in work already. I can't keep up with my

projects and daily operational work. Why should I put myself out there, go out on a limb when I don't have time to adequately prepare?"

7. *They won't let me.* When asked why more BAs don't do business cases, we often hear the emphasis on *"they"*—the powers that be, the people with authority—"won't let me." To me, the words "they won't let me" show helplessness. "They" shows total lack of empowerment. But where does empowerment come from? Do we wait for someone with authority to give us a slice of authority? Can someone else ever empower us? We don't think so. We think maybe they can create an environment where we feel empowered, but that's very different from empowering another person. We can use our expertise and our leadership skills to influence others without ever being formally empowered by someone else.

> **TIP**
>
> If you have built good relationships, if you are prepared, and if you keep the organization's goals and objectives in mind at all times, it's easier to be courageous than if any of the ingredients are missing.

Keys to Being Courageous

The real key to being courageous is to remember the Influencing Formula. If you have built good relationships, if you are prepared, and if you keep the organization's goals and objectives in mind at all times, it's easier to be courageous than if any of the ingredients are missing.

1. *Be prepared.* It is far easier to be courageous when we are prepared, which gives us the confidence we need to recommend the right thing.

Being prepared prevents our ideas from being outlandish because we know what "outlandish" means in our organization. We know what will and will not work. We do not care if our ideas seem "obvious" because we understand the problem and we recommend the solution that best solves that problem—and the simpler the solution, the better.

> ### Seven Keys to Being Courageous
> 1. Be prepared.
> 2. Be confident.
> 3. Be credible.
> 4. Establish good relationships.
> 5. Recommend the right thing.
> 6. Avoid personal agendas.
> 7. Gain support.

2. *Be confident.* It's so easy to say "be confident," but if we tend towards diffidence, confidence may not be easy to obtain. We have found that some people who appear confident, even arrogant, often lack confidence. We have also found that being prepared provides us with confidence. When we are not prepared, we might speak confidently, but when questioned, we stumble. So the key to our confidence is being prepared.

3. *Be credible.* The more credibility we have built up, based on our character and our competence, the easier it is to be courageous. Having credibility makes it easier to enter a meeting and speak out, to disagree, to state an opinion, or provide a recommendation based on our experience.

Many of us cannot build credibility immediately. We are either outside consultants going into a variety of organizations or simply new enough in our organization and have no history relating to our character or competence.

We might have been recommended or we might have shown our portfolio of past project successes, but each time we start anew, we need to establish our credibility.

What can we do to overcome this obstacle? It helps to tell stories, not just of our past successes, but our failures and why what we tried didn't work. India's first woman prime minister, Indira Gandhi, once said, "Trust one who has been through it," and going through it means that we've both succeeded and failed. We need to be specific enough to be able to explain why things work and don't work and what causes the success and failure.

4. *Establish good relationships.* We cannot build trust without good relationships. Again, those of us who are external consultants do not always have the luxury of taking the time to establish good relationships. Yet we need to do exactly that. We need to rely on our sponsors because they are the ones who funded our effort, and they have the most to lose if we fail. We'll have to remember all the ways to build trust quickly, such as making realistic commitments and meeting them, communicating bad news, etc. Remember the importance of communicating to match the style of the other people's styles in individual and group meetings, as well as the importance of communicating in a style that promotes rather than destroys trust.

5. *Advising and recommending the right thing*, not deciding. Another courage-builder is knowing that the ultimate decision rests elsewhere. When we've done our homework and have provided solid advice, we've done our job. We do not need or even want to make the final decision. That is not our role.

When we inappropriately play the role of business decision-maker, we risk getting involved in territorial battles that will be hard to win and might lessen our confidence.

6. *Avoiding personal agendas.* Remember that having courage is helped by doing the right thing for the organization. We have known people who have had their own agendas and "sold" their agenda as the right thing for the organization. We recommend the opposite. Instead of starting with what we want and making it fit the organization, we need to start with what the organization needs. The trick is to know what your organization needs. Some of our clients work in organizations that don't publish their goals and objectives, or the goals are so broad, such as increasing revenues, that all actions might be interpreted as aligning with those goals.

   One of the most difficult aspects to avoiding personal agendas is when our agenda aligns with our business unit or division but conflicts with other business units or divisions. We all want to do the right thing, but what happens when our goals are aligned with our government agency, but the agency's goals conflict with our personal goals? In that example, we need to find the courage to take the time to ensure all goals are aligned. Again, focusing on the right thing for the organization rather than our own agendas can provide lots of courage.

7. *Gaining support* requires the ability to sell our ideas, and we provide tips for gaining support in the next section.

Five Tips for Gaining Support

Once we have decided on a recommendation, we need to have the courage to sell it, but that won't be possible if we don't gain the support of others.

> **Five Tips for Gaining Support**
>
> 1. Believe in your recommendation.
> 2. Meet individually.
> 3. Overcome objections.
> 4. Provide plan for implementing.
> 5. Ask for their support.

There are many ingredients that go into gaining the support of others. Here are a few really important ones.

1. *Believe in the emotional value and benefits of our recommendation.* In addition to being thoroughly prepared with quantifiable benefits of our recommendation, we need to get an emotional understanding of our recommendation's benefits. It is also essential that we have a strong desire that our recommendation be supported by as many stakeholders as possible. To achieve not only approval, but support and actual commitment, the emotional value that we place on our recommendations must be transferred to the stakeholders.

   Why? Remember that stakeholders say they will support you based on *logic*, but they actually commit based on *emotions*.

   As an example, Elizabeth was working on a project once that had no clear *quantifiable* benefits. Nevertheless, the project sponsor made it clear that the project would allow the organization to compete in the marketplace with its chief competitor.

   The sponsor was emotionally attached to the project and could sell it to the senior executives because of its emotional value.

There may be stakeholders who, for a variety of reasons, do not want to buy our recommendations. There is nothing wrong with working through our champions and having them help bring reluctant stakeholders on board.

2. *Meet individually with stakeholders.* In order to assess a stakeholder's level of support and commitment, we need to meet with them individually rather than in a group. Meeting in a group poses the risk of not getting a true assessment of how supportive the individual is. The group dynamics, as well as the interrelationships of the people in the group, can have a major effect on the level of support. Most of us are much more likely to agree with an idea or recommendation if our bosses also agree. If a superior voices opposition, we will assess whether providing our support is worth the risk of disagreeing with that person. We have learned to put extra time into projects to meet individually both before and after meetings with certain key stakeholders. There are those whose support must be assessed and hopefully attained before the large facilitated meetings take place. There are others who say they will provide their support during a meeting, but when they go back to their desks, they change their minds. Meeting individually provides a way to bring reluctant stakeholders on board.

3. *Determine and overcome objections.* When we have a recommendation and are ready to present it, we don't send it in an impersonal email and wait passively for a response. We need to meet with the stakeholders. We don't want our recommendations lost or forgotten in the decision-maker's low priority pile. And we do not want to hear, "I'm busy right now. I'll review it if I have time." We need to schedule time, live or virtually, so that during the proposal each appropriate stakeholder can raise objections. We need to

listen actively to those objections. We need to address each concern. We need to find reasons for them to want to buy our recommendation.

4. *Make it easy for them—provide a plan.* It is far easier to garner support when we provide support on how to implement the recommendation. We presented this important "I" step with the SARIE tool in the Chapter 6. We have found many stakeholders who respond favorably to an idea but balk at the idea of having to implement it. Implementing new processes involves disruption and can seem overwhelming. When we make it easy for them to implement, they are more likely to buy into our recommendation. Providing a detailed implementation plan with fairly narrow tasks makes the implementation understandable and less overwhelming, thereby increasing the chance they will support our recommendation.

5. *Ask for their support.* In order to effectively influence, we need the ability to ask for the "sale." We can't sell without closing the deal. In other words, a critical factor for selling our recommendation is to be able to "ask for the order."

   Simply presenting the benefits of our recommendation isn't enough. We must be able to ask the "prospect" to take action, and that action must include a commitment to helping it succeed. After the "buyer" takes action, we must then deliver on what we have proposed. We don't want the stakeholder to be unhappy and have buyer's remorse. In our business we have learned the hard way that simply proposing without "selling" is not enough.

P.E.T.A.L.-ing the "sale"

"Selling" our recommendation means we need to close the "sale," and "P.E.T.A.L." the recommendation. That doesn't mean pushing it. When we P.E.T.A.L. a recommendation, we follow five simple steps.

1. Clearly state the PROBLEM, pain, opportunity, or threat. If our recommendation is not approved, it may be that we have not stated the real problem or uncovered enough pain. We have discussed the importance of thoroughly understanding the business problem and associated pain or gain in Chapter 4, Influential Preparation.

2. We need to be ENTHUSIASTIC about our recommendation and deliver it in an engaging way. If we are tentative about our recommendation, or if we seem timid or, worse yet, bored, we will have a hard time convincing other stakeholders that they should be excited. However, if we have a passionate belief in the recommendation, stakeholders are more apt to respond positively.

3. We need to give some stakeholders TIME to consider their objections. Although we believe in our recommendation because we've done our homework and are confident and credible, although we want a decision immediately, and although we believe we've made such a good case that we can "close the sale" immediately, we do need to give stakeholders time to consider what we have presented. If we push too hard, we run the risk that our stakeholders will initially accept the recommendation but then later change their minds. It is far better for us to encourage stakeholders to raise their objections sooner rather than later. We do not want them to approve a recommendation quickly and experience regrets about approving it. It's far better not to rush the decision. Doing our stakeholder analysis (Chapter

5) will help us determine which stakeholders will probably need more time to think about our recommendation before approving it.

4. Ensure that we get input from **ALL** appropriate stakeholders. So often we get input from those who support us. Sometimes we even avoid seeking approval from stakeholders we think will not support and might even oppose our recommendation. However, it is important to find out who supports us and who doesn't. We will never close the sale if we only get input from our known champions.

5. We need to be prepared to LEAVE if the decision has been not been made or has been made to reject the recommendation. During a meeting, it is counterproductive to force a decision. Not receiving immediate approval does not mean we have failed. It does not mean that we should forget about the recommendation that we prepared so well. We do not go away discouraged. We listen carefully to the objections, answer what we can in the meeting, and leave to better prepare our recommendation and adjust our process for gaining approval.

P.E.T.A.L.-ing our recommendation

P   Solve real Problems

E   Deliver with Enthusiasm

T   Allow enough Time

A   Involve All stakeholders

L   Be prepared to Leave and try again

Table 21 is a checklist for gaining approval for our recommendations.

Checklist for Gaining Approval		
Item	Y/N	Comments
Does the recommendation solve a real business problem?		
Have you identified the associated pain?		
Do you have a passionate belief in the recommendation?		
Have you delivered the recommendation with enthusiasm and in an engaging way?		
Have you done your communication homework by having one-on-ones before presenting to a large audience?		
Have you leveraged champions to get reluctant stakeholders on board?		
Are you prepared to let the decision go if not approved?		

TABLE 21: Checklist for Presenting Our Recommendations

In summary, we need to gain support for our recommendation as the last important key to being courageous. To gain support, we need to believe in our recommendations and the emotional, not just the logical, benefit. We need to hold individual meetings with affected stakeholders to assess their support and get their commitment. It is important to find out who supports and who opposes our recommendation and the issues, or objections, they have before we can resolve those issues. Once we determine them, we need to work at how they can be resolved to the stakeholders' satisfaction.

One common objection is the disruption of implementing the recommendation. By providing a realistic implementation plan, we can alleviate the anxiety associated with implementing the recommendation. Finally, we need to actively ask for stakeholder support and commitment to making it work.

The Trusted Advisor and Courage

So what does courage really mean for us as trusted advisors? In our role as the trusted advisor, we need to have the courage to provide advice. We keep emphasizing that as trusted advisors we need to recommend the right thing for the project and for the organization. For example, we have asked a variety of presentation and seminar participants whether they write business cases for potential projects. We have found that business cases are not completed in many organizations. When asked why, many said that it was not an accepted practice in their organization.

If the organization where we work doesn't want to spend time doing business cases, would we simply ignore management and develop business cases? No, that would be rash and apt to break trust. First, we would determine if developing business cases were a real need in the organization. We'd find out the problems and pains associated with not having business cases. We'd look at costs of doing versus not doing business cases and the benefits of each.

In other words, what we would do is put together a detailed recommendation, a SARIE, for why it's in the best interest of the organization to complete or continue not completing business

"Be the change you wish to see in the world."

MAHATMA GANDHI

cases. We'd put together a business case for doing business cases.

We also need the courage to listen. As Winston Churchill said, "Courage is what it takes to stand up and speak; courage is also what it takes to sit down and listen."[12] We have discussed techniques for active listening in Chapter 7.

Courage, WIIFM, and WIIFO

Project professionals often use the expression WIIFM (what's in it for me) when referring to a way to explain benefits to reluctant stakeholders. Explaining what's in it for the individual is a technique used to garner the support of those stakeholders who have not bought into our projects. We all need to understand the benefits of the work we do to ourselves. As project managers and business analysts, it's also important to ensure that the goals of the project team members and business stakeholders align with the goals of the project and organization. If there's a gap, or mismatch, we need to probe more deeply to see if such an alignment is possible. If not, other organizational support may be needed.

What gives us courage is when we know that the project and everyone involved with the project will be more successful if it helps the organization meet its goals. What helps the organization helps us in every way. It's in our own best interest. Therefore, when we can articulate not just WIIFM, but also WIIFO—what's in it for the organization—we know we'll be more successful. It's far easier to be courageous when we're protecting ourselves too! We like to add to the Mahatma Gandhi quote "Be the change you wish to see in the world"—be the change you want to see in your organization.

Summary

- In this chapter, we defined courage, reviewed barriers to courage, provided tips to being courageous, and looked at the role of courage in providing recommendations as the trusted advisor.
- We discussed tips for selling our recommendation and gaining support.
- And, we introduced the idea of P.E.T.A.L.-ing our recommendations.

1   Rushworth M. Kidder and Martha Bracy. "Moral Courage, A White Paper," *Institute for Global Ethics,* accessed July 15, 2012, http://ww2.faulkner.edu/admin/websites/jfarrell/moral_courage_11-03-2001.pdf.

2   Stephen M.R. Covey. *The SPEED of Trust: The One Thing That Changes Everything* (New York: Free Press, 2008), 64.

3   David H. Maister, et al. *The Trusted Advisor.* (New York: Simon & Schuster, 2000), 135.

4   Kidder, ibid.

5   Dictionary.com, accessed July 09, 2012,http://dictionary.reference.com/browse/courage.

6   Wiktionary, accessed July 09, 2012,http://en.wiktionary.org/wiki/courage.

7   Merriam-Webster.com. accessed July 09, 2012, http://www.merriam-webster.com/dictionary/courage.

8   Wiktionary, accessed July 09, 2012, http://en.wiktionary.org/wiki/courage.

9   Elaine Sternberg. *Just Business: Business Ethics in Action.* London: Little, Brown and Company, 1994, pp. 82-83, accessed July 15, 2012, [as viewed in Rushworth M. Kidder and Martha Bracy. "Moral Courage, A White Paper," Institute for Global Ethics http://ww2.faulkner.edu/admin/websites/jfarrell/moral_courage_11-03-2001.pdf].

10 Harper Lee. To Kill a Mockingbird, 1960, accessed July 15, 2012, http://www.quotationspage.com/quote/1765.html.

11 Robert N. Van Wyk. *Introduction to Ethics* (New York: St. Martin's Press, 1990), p. 175, accessed July 15, 2012, [as viewed in Rushworth M. Kidder and Martha Bracy. "Moral Courage, A White Paper", *Institute for Global Ethics* http://ww2.faulknr.edu/admin/websites/jfarrell/moral_courage_11-03-2001.pdf].

12 Winston Churchill Quotes, BrainyQuote. accessed July 15, 2012, http://www.brainyquote.com/quotes/authors/w/winston_churchill.html#skgZah3ARWSQoS2d.99.

09

Influencing Difficult Stakeholders

"We are constantly being put to the test by trying circumstances and difficult people and problems not necessarily of our own making."

TERRY BROOKS
AMERICAN AUTHOR OF FANTASY FICTION

It takes courage to deal with difficult stakeholders. As described in the section on barriers (Chapter 8), we have heard reports of intimidation, bullying, sabotage, and passive-aggressive behavior. There are risks involved no matter how we handle these situations. We need courage regardless of whether we deal with this behavior directly, avoid it, or work through others to handle it. Despite the risks, we need to work with these stakeholders because the right thing to do for the project and for the organization is to handle difficult stakeholders professionally and courteously.

What makes difficult stakeholders difficult?

There are innumerable reasons why difficult stakeholders appear hard to get along with. There might even be times, although rare, that we encounter stakeholders with psychological problems, and it is most likely beyond our abilities to make them happy. Most often, however, stakeholders are not really difficult but, instead, frustrated with the current situation. When this frustration is related to our projects, there are many ways we can improve our relationship with these stakeholders. We need to realize that often frustration is born from unmet expectations, which cause stakeholders to act in ways that make them seem difficult to us.

Table 22 presents common reasons for unmet expectations, a further explanation of these reasons, and tips for dealing with them to help prevent our stakeholders' negative reactions.

Reason for Unmet Expectations	Explanation	What We Can Do
Waiting too long for their new product or service. The business benefit that they envisioned has not been attained	When we start a project of any size, it's almost impossible to predict with any certainty how large it is. There are many pieces and interfaces, to say nothing of effects on current processes and information. Even if plans and actuals are provided on a regular basis, stakeholders can be frustrated by how long the project lasts.	Divide the project into smaller pieces, plan and track against more milestones, and deliver smaller features and functionality that provide more business value sooner than delivering when all features are complete.
Not understanding feature dependency	Simply delivering high-priority functionality first doesn't always work. There are often dependencies that require pieces to be in place before other high-value features are completed. For example, getting timely information might be the most important feature to a sponsor. However, that information needs to be captured before it can be reported, so there is a dependency constraint placed on implementing the high-priority item. It is essential to have the appropriate stakeholders involved in prioritizing the features and equally essential that we explain these types of constraints in business terms so the stakeholders understand.	We need to explain dependencies in a way that is complete but simple to understand and in business terms. We also need to ensure that the stakeholders understand their role in determining business value and setting priorities—they are accountable for those decisions.

Reason for Unmet Expectations	Explanation	What We Can Do
Not understanding the processes used to build the product	While business stakeholders do not need to understand the fundamentals of every development life cycle, methodology, process, or method used to develop products, they do need to understand the ramifications of using them. They need to know the risks as well as the benefits. For example, many stakeholders have heard of the benefits of using Agile methods, such as on Agile projects there is no misconceptions, such as on Agile projects there is no documentation, or with Agile methods everything is done quickly and there is no planning required. They think that Agile means they do not need to be involved. When these stakeholders become part of an Agile project and are asked to own the product requirements, including priority and changes, they can become frustrated.	Before organizations embark on new development processes, such as the use of Agile methods, they need to understand both the benefits and the costs, as well as the impact to the organization, including the business and technical areas. These types of decisions should not be made in a vacuum. Countless executives have ordered the use of Agile methods without understanding the cultural impacts. Our clients and presentation participants cite example after example of how these efforts have been unsuccessful.

Reason for Unmet Expectations	Explanation	What We Can Do
Promised dates missed or not provided; the "Oh this won't take too long" syndrome	One constant throughout the decades is the "OOPS" factor. When we estimate, we tend to be Overly optimistic, we tend to Overlook some important stakeholders, we tend to ignore our Plan (if there is one), and we tend to stay on the Surface without getting to the level of detail required to understand the scope of our work and how long that effort will take.	Remember that it's easier to estimate smaller pieces than whole projects or even project phases. When we estimate by requirement, it's easier to see how many requirements we can deliver in a given time frame. And it's easier to track against plan. Another good practice is time boxing after estimating size. Time boxing is about setting specific time frames, such as two weeks, determining how much will fit into each time box based on the estimates, and making a commitment to complete that amount of work in that amount of time. With time boxing, the scope needs to be fixed. Agile methods, such as Scrum, use this approach, which proves invaluable in setting expectations.

Reason for Unmet Expectations	Explanation	What We Can Do
Products delivered with defect(s)	Sometimes project managers forget to set metrics for project success and make the assumption that they need to finish their projects on time and within budgets, even if it means delivering with defects. Although on some projects sponsors care more about delivering on time than delivering a defect-free product, most often the business becomes frustrated when all our projects have defects. Also, when we have delivered defective products in the past, our stakeholders might be holding on to frustrations from past projects.	Explain project constraints to the sponsor and negotiate the acceptance criteria to be used to measure project success. Communicate these decisions to the other project stakeholders, getting their input as well. If there are discrepancies between the sponsor's measures of success and those of other stakeholders, we need to facilitate sessions to bring all stakeholders to consensus. It is important to remember, however, that the sponsor is the ultimate decision-maker.

Reason for Unmet Expectations	Explanation	What We Can Do
Feelings of powerless in relation to other project stakeholders	We project professionals feel powerless so often that it is hard to imagine that some of our stakeholders feel the same way. When we work on cross-functional projects where we need input from a variety of different stakeholders, not all of whom work for the project sponsor, it is hard to give equal attention and priority to all stakeholders. We've had stakeholders ask us why they get more requirements in the first release.	We cannot ignore business SMEs who have less of a stake in the project than others. There are usually too many unknown and unintentional consequences. As noted above, ultimately the sponsor gets to decide. However, sponsors do not want to be dragged into every dispute among stakeholders, so as trusted advisors, we need to do what we can to bring people to consensus. We need to understand all sides well enough to recommend a solution that will bring the greatest accord.
Trust has been broken	Stakeholders can appear difficult when they don't trust us. As discussed in the Building Trust chapter, once trust has been broken, particularly trust related to one's character, it is hard to restore. It will take time and may not be possible.	As we said earlier, we can only do what we can do. We may not be able to change the situation significantly. However, we can take the initiative to communicate and to be sincere about cleaning up our trust issues.

Reason for Unmet Expectations	Explanation	What We Can Do
Difficulties with somebody or something else	Sometimes stakeholders can appear difficult simply because they are frustrated with difficult people and/or technology that is hard to use or not working. Sometimes stakeholders are not feeling well and take it out on us. There are many reasons unrelated to us that can cause others to be cranky or short or appear frustrated with us.	We need to try and not take it personally and to remain professional at all times. We also need to remember that timing is important, so if someone is frustrated, and that frustration is not related to us, perhaps we need to talk to them some other time.
Feeling dismissed	We have seen some technical experts talking down to business stakeholders. There is sometimes a technical arrogance that makes business people feel unimportant or even stupid. On the other hand, we have encountered some technical stakeholders who also feel dismissed and taken for granted. They have been assigned to multiple projects. When they express valid concerns and risks, they are told to be quiet and build what the customer wants. Good technical professionals are invaluable and should be used as trusted advisors in their own right. Whether part of the business or technical areas, everyone wants to be kept informed throughout the project.	We need to ensure that we always communicate with respect, actively listen to concerns, solicit their input, and keep stakeholders informed.

TABLE 22: Types of Difficult Stakeholders

What do they want? Stakeholders who appear difficult may want the following:

They want what they've requested. And they don't want to wait months or years to get it. They don't understand why project delays occur and get frustrated when we talk about delays, particularly when we emphasize that delays are not our fault.

- **They want it when they need it**. Sponsors, after all, do pay for the projects, so why shouldn't they get to say what they want, how much they are willing to spend, and when they want it? We need to do a better job explaining the project constraints before the project management plan is complete. They need to understand that although they have ultimate decision-making about what they want when they want it, there are costs. Very few sponsors we've encountered have unlimited budgets. It is our job to explain the impacts of adding more scope without extending the time or adding to the budget.

- **They want their jobs made easier, not harder**. So many of us feel pressure to complete our work. More and more of us work extended hours each week trying to keep up with our workload. When our stakeholders are asked to participate on projects, they expect relief, not more work. They often perceive us as roadblocks to getting their jobs done. New products and processes often make jobs harder than what is familiar to them, particularly at first. New processes and automated systems will take time to learn, to say nothing of the time to provide input on what's happening today (the "as-is") and what changes are needed (the "to-be").

- **They want choices. Most of us want options.** We don't want, and may even resent, others telling us what to do. When we build a home and we notice missing features, even if we were the ones who forgot to include them, we don't want to be told that we can't have that feature or that it's too late in the process. We want choices of how to best incorporate the feature, how that feature impacts other features, what it will cost, and how much time it will add to the total cost. How many of us have told stakeholders that it was too late in the process to make a change? Sadly, we are guilty. When we built our first home, we added many new features and knew we would need to pay for the changes. However, one of our stated requirements was electrical outlets in the living room floor. We wanted to be able to plug in lamps and computers without having cords snaking across the room. This requirement was registered in the formal set of specifications. During a walk-through after the wood floors were installed, we noticed that these floor plugs were missing. When we talked to the builder, he said we had no choice at that point. He was terribly sorry that the requirement was missed, and he would give us a refund of a couple of dollars, but there was no recourse. To this day, we still talk about the missing floor plugs.

- **They want recommendations and advice.** We go to lawyers for advice. We go to doctors for advice. We expect interior designers, financial planners, dentists, builders, and remodelers all to provide us with advice. We want to hear about benefits, risks, and issues, which is what our stakeholders want from us. When we make business or technical decisions rather than providing recommendations, we can trigger difficult behavior. How would we react if our house builder said to us that "I have already picked out your flooring or wall colors," or similarly if our lawyers said, "I have added beneficiaries to your estate." We would be cranky too!

- **They want opportunities to provide their input.** In prior chapters, we discussed the pitfalls of delivering a product or service without getting input from our stakeholders. It is not difficult to imagine the reaction of stakeholders when handed some kind of product or service that they were expected to use but about which they had little or no knowledge. It's hard enough to use a new system, for example, when we've been involved in the decision-making. Imagine how we'd react to being handed a new automated system and told, "You need to start using this new system. We're turning off the old system next week. Don't worry. You'll love this new system." We would certainly become difficult. We remember all the new versions of Windows that we have had to learn over time. We were certainly frustrated when some of the earlier versions took away functionality that we had gotten used to and even liked. No wonder stakeholders get frustrated when we don't solicit their input.

> **TIP**
>
> Difficult stakeholders want:
>
> • What they've asked for...
>
> • ...when they need it
>
> • To have work made easier, not harder
>
> • Choices
>
> • Input
>
> • Acknowledgement

- **They want acknowledgement.** When stakeholders provide their input, we need to acknowledge it. We do not need to agree with it, but we do need to sincerely thank them for their input. Remember that "yes" does not necessarily mean that we agree. It means that, yes, we have heard and understand and that we will take that input seriously.

Difficult behavior can put us off balance. Some of our classes include role play interviews with difficult stakeholders. It is amazing to see over and over how students who do a great job mimicking an intimidating stakeholder can throw the student interviewer off track. Sometimes interviewers get so flustered they never seem to recover. Most often when confronted with a difficult stakeholder, we withdraw. We might stop inviting difficult stakeholders to meetings, which exacerbates the issues stated above. For example, when we encounter difficult personalities and stop inviting them to meetings, they become frustrated about not being acknowledged or not providing input. This frustration can grow, and the vicious cycle continues.

Difficult stakeholders can demean and intimidate us. In some organizations, this behavior is expected. In others, it is forbidden. For those unlucky enough to have to face intimidation and bullying, we need courage to handle it. That courage might take the form of discussing the behavior with the intimidator, or it might mean leaving the organization. Both options require intestinal fortitude, but ignoring it is cowardice.

At the root of some difficult behavior is fear. What about our projects causes this fear? *Table 23* shows common causes of fear leading to difficult behavior and what we can do about it.

Afraid that the new product or service will:	Explanation	What we can do
Change my processes, and I like what I have	All of us are familiar with the expressions "If it ain't broke, don't fix it" and "I've always done it this way." It's hard to change what we are used to and what works for us. It's more than being stuck in a routine. We know how to get results a certain way and there are risks with changing it.	We need to understand the current process and all the variations and exceptions. We need to graphically show all anomalies. We need to show all the different ways different stakeholders perform the same process, whether the steps are performed in a different order, not performed at all, or done differently. The graphical process model or map is a great way to show that new processes are needed. We also need to make sure that these stakeholders participate in designing the new processes.
Eliminate my job	This is a real fear, and unfortunately, sometimes jobs are eliminated with new processes and systems.	If the organization needs to eliminate jobs and we are working on projects to do just that, we need to be transparent. We need to work with the appropriate organizational resources to communicate the organization's goals to the affected stakeholders.[1]
Impede or slow my current process	Stakeholders are afraid that the new products, particularly new systems or processes, will eliminate the workarounds and shortcuts that they have developed. They are concerned that new processes will take longer to produce the required outputs.	Ensure we get input from affected stakeholders on their current processes and provide training on the new ones. The project team needs to be familiar with the systems that they use currently. We need to understand the impacts of replacing what they currently have and ensure that they are aware of and ready for the changes.

Afraid that the new product or service will:	Explanation	What we can do
Take too much time to learn or support	We can provide training on the changes, but the stakeholders fear that they will need to keep up with their current workload while learning how to use/support/sell, etc., the new product or service.	Raise this as an issue as soon as it surfaces. We on the project team cannot resolve this issue ourselves. We can, however, get the appropriate people together to address the issue.
Take away familiar tools and replace them with new ones that will be harder to use	"You mean I'll have to give up my spreadsheet?!" Familiar tools are comfortable, and most of us are uncomfortable giving up what works for us.	Explain the pain relating to the old way of doing things and the benefits of the new tools. Explain what's in it for both the individual and the organization.
Mean that I am no longer the expert	In Chapter 1, we discussed forms of power and showed that Expert power was strong and long-lasting. If stakeholders have to throw away what they've been doing and pick up something new, they will lose their expertise and, along with it, their power.	Explain that learning new tools provides new experience and expertise. It is a way to learn new skills and help prevent the "dinosaur syndrome," in which skills and people become obsolete.

TABLE 23: Stakeholder Fears

The S.A.F.E Model

What can we do when we are bullied or intimated and don't know whether to get angry or crawl away (the old fight or flight syndrome)? We can follow the S.A.F.E. Model.[2]

In short, the S.A.F.E. Model is a way to calm ourselves and look at the situation unemotionally rather than focusing on the difficult stakeholder. It is a model for allowing objective data to replace negative emotions. *Figure 29* describes this model.

S.A.F.E. Model

Helps us be Courageous

Stabilize	*Acknowledge*	*Focus*	*Evaluate*
• Yourself	• Emotion	• Situation	• Data
• Situation	• Misunderstanding	• Stakeholder	• Follow through
	• Responsa	• Real problem	• Internal radar
		• Separate people from problem	• Verify/validate

FIGURE 29: S.A.F.E. Model

- **STABILIZE.** When difficult stakeholders knock us off balance, we need to get out of react mode quickly. We need to take time and recognize that this is a situation that might not bring out our best behavior. We need to get ourselves grounded in order to respond appropriately. The age-old advice to count to ten or take a deep breath is sound.

- **ACKNOWLEDGE.** A more stable situation will allow us to acknowledge our emotions, as well as try to recognize those of the difficult stakeholders. Are they angry? Frustrated? Annoyed? Once we concentrate on emotions, ours and theirs, we can analyze the steps that led to the situation and acknowledge our role in the conflict.

- **FOCUS.** Next we need to focus on the actual problem, what objectively happened, not just what we think occurred. We also need to understand the context leading up to the situation. We need to be sure not to get into the blame or internal name-calling mode. It is not productive to think, "He's such a jerk. He always explodes at the least thing." And we need to think about the problem at hand rather than the person causing the problem.

- **EVALUATE.** The final step is to mentally review what actually occurred. We need to examine the actual words and non-verbals in the exchange and examine what was really said, not imagined.

Table 24 is a checklist of questions to ask ourselves as we step through the S.A.F.E. phases.

Phase	Questions to ask ourselves
Stabilize	• What is happening now? • How can I keep from reacting negatively?
Acknowledge	• What emotion are they displaying? • What am I feeling right now? • What did I say to trigger their negative reaction? • What was my response to the situation? • What did they do in response to what I did?
Focus	• How have our past interactions affected what just happened? • How have they reacted in the past? • How have I reacted in the past?

Phase	Questions to ask ourselves
Evaluate	• What actually happened vs. what I think happened • What actual words were spoken? • What were the specific, observable non-verbals, and what did they really communicate? • How do I know what was communicated? Is it my interpretation, or did it actually occur?

TABLE 24: S.A.F.E. Checklist

How to Be Wildly Unsuccessful at Managing Difficult Stakeholders

We've all encountered them—the bureaucrats who follow processes because they've been told to or because they're comfortable with the routine. They don't like exceptions. Not long ago we were taking an international trip. We had to check luggage at the airport, so we presented our passport to the ticket agent. He keyed something into the computer and said, "There's a problem with your reservation. I can get you to your first stop. But you'll have to check with the ticket agent in Sydney, Australia." We were reluctant to travel around the world only to find the problem couldn't be resolved, so we asked about the nature of the problem. He didn't know but asked the agent next to him. She clearly couldn't be bothered to answer. She, of course, had to help her line of customers. He kept looking at the long line of customers waiting to check in and kept telling us to go away. We refused to go and asked to talk to a manager. He then disappeared for quite some time. In the meantime, a supervisor walked by, and we asked for her help. It turns out the original agent forgot to scan our passports. This supervisor scanned them, and we were on our way. It was clear to us that the agents were measured on their "productivity," which meant how many customers they could get through per hour, rather than on helping customers.

There are common mistakes that many of us make in dealing with our project stakeholders. These mistakes are presented in *Table 25*.

Common Mistakes	Example
Deny or dismiss their feedback	You don't understand...
Blame something/somebody else for their problem	Hey, it's not my fault. Operations won't let us implement on that date.
Label them as "difficult" without trying to understand the problem	Oh, you know Joe. He's a chronic complainer. No one takes him seriously. Jane's no better. She always makes excuses when she shows up late for meetings, if she bothers to show up at all.
Interrupt them with an answer	Forgive me for interrupting, but the reason you can't have this requirement is that it does not trace to the project objectives.
Shove them off on someone else	You'll have to talk to the sponsor about that. She's the one who will have to make that decision.
Tell them where they can go to get help	Sorry, I can't help you with that one. Why don't you try the database analyst?
Don't deal with the problem in a timely manner	I'll get back to you ASAP, which means the bottom of the pile.

Common Mistakes	Example
Explain your process before listening	Before you go any further, I need to tell you about our requirements process.
View most clients as "dumb users" who don't know what they want	That's not what you said last week. You told me that you didn't need that feature. We'll never get this system developed if you keep changing your mind.
Enforce a strict methodology	I'm sorry, but I can't tell you how big the project is. We don't provide any estimates until we've completed the analysis phase.
When stakeholders are wrong, be sure to tell them but never admit when you're wrong	Actually, the current system does have that feature. Maybe you haven't been trained how to use it, but it's there.

TABLE 25: Common Mistakes With Difficult Stakeholders

How can we deal with difficult stakeholders?

We need to be sure that they feel significant. We need to respect and recognize them. Instead of ignoring them during a requirements workshop, for example, actively solicit their input. Many difficult stakeholders feel dismissed or feel that their input is not being valued. We need to treat them with respect. (Yes, even when they are being difficult.) We need to acknowledge their contributions, even when we don't agree with them.

We need to actively listen and understand their concerns. That means, of course, we need to practice active listening as described in Chapter 7, Consultative Questioning.

We need to be sure that we are keeping them informed. With difficult stakeholders, we need to make an effort to share information and be transparent. We need to act fairly and not play favorites, and as far as possible, get to know them. We have found that some of the most intimidating stakeholders turn out to be the most interesting and fun at informal company gatherings.

We need to be the trusted advisor, providing options and recommendations and ultimately products and services that work for them.

Difficult Stakeholders Come in Different Sizes and Shapes

We rarely hear of facilitated meetings and workshops that did *not* have disruptive, difficult stakeholders. Almost all project professionals who facilitate meetings have to deal with them. For some reason, it seems that meetings tend to bring out the worst in difficult stakeholders. Yet most of us project managers and business analysts are called on to be facilitators. How can we handle these difficult stakeholders? By using what we call the BID Model. BID stands for:

Behavior: What is the *observable* behavior of the difficult stakeholder? What is the person *doing specifically* that is causing the disruption or conflict?

Impact: What is the impact on the team, group, and facilitator? What are the consequences of the behavior? Why does it matter that they are doing this?

Development: What are the steps necessary for development of more appropriate behavior?

Table 26 lists some common difficult stakeholder types; their observable behaviors; the impact on the team, group, and facilitator; and the development steps to improve the situation.

Type	Behavior and Impact	Development (Tips to Improve the Situation)
Comedian	**Behavior.** Disrupts discussion with jokes, sarcasm, or wisecracks, often directed to someone in particular but loud enough for everyone to hear. Asks "What's the matter, don't you have a sense of humor?" Constantly seeks attention. **Impact.** Participants feel dismissed and can become defensive. Slows the process.	• Discuss impact on team and other stakeholders directly with them. • Discuss individually; try to determine root cause of disruption. • Specifically seek joker's contribution. • Take control—summarize and refocus team or meeting participants.
Nay-Sayer	**Behavior.** Complains about new ways of doing their job. They say, "If it ain't broke, don't fix it" or "We've always done it this way" or "This will never work." **Impact.** Participants become discouraged and may stop participating.	• Meet individually to uncover the real issues. • Refocus on organization and project objectives and what's in it for them. • Work with them to help them restate their concerns as risks and into "I wish I knew how to" statements.

Type	Behavior and Impact	Development (Tips to Improve the Situation)
Initial Rejecter	**Behavior.** Unlike the nay-sayer, the initial rejecter pipes up with valid reasons why "it will never work." **Impact.** Participants join the bandwagon and concentrate on issues and risks rather than benefits.	• Work with them to help them restate their concerns as risks and into "I wish I knew how to" statements. Have them state their concerns as risks. • Take concerns seriously. These are likely real issues that need to be addressed. • Remember that initial rejecters will most likely be strong supporters once their concerns have been addressed.
Attacker	**Behavior.** Criticizes everything and everyone. Intimidates and bullies. **Impact.** Participants feel unsafe and shut down. No real work gets done.	• Meet individually to uncover the real issues. • Discuss impact of their behavior on the team, yourself, and other stakeholders directly with them. • Ask for their input in how to relieve their frustration. • In meetings, use others to widen discussion and dilute negativity.

Type	Behavior and Impact	Development (Tips to Improve the Situation)
Persistent Talker	**Behavior.** Has extensive views on everything! **Impact.** Participants shut down or become frustrated or argumentative. Little work gets completed.	• Set expectations at the beginning of the meeting. • Reinforce the meeting objectives and desired outcome. • If in a group meeting, enforce ground rules. • 5-minute rule. • One voice at a time.
Reluctant Talker	**Behavior.** Fails to contribute **Impact.** The facilitator fails to reach the desired outcome of the meeting.	• Define ground rules for participation and get group to endorse them. • Seek contributions, but do not pressure. May need to get input during 1:1. • Conduct one-on-ones before and after larger group meetings. • Reward contributions.

Type	Behavior and Impact	Development (Tips to Improve the Situation)
Persistent Questioner	**Behavior.** Appears to seek understanding but delays and derails meeting with constant questions. **Impact.** The facilitator fails to reach the desired outcome of the meeting.	• Use Parking Lot, which is a list of topics to be discussed at a later date. • Target questioner with questions—e.g., what are your ideas here…? • Look for hidden agenda. • Briefly recap and summarize. • Avoid going over old ground. • Call for time out and summarize for individual.
Know-It-All	**Behavior.** These types have seen it all, done it all, and feel the session is beneath them. Often ridicules ideas; may have hidden agenda. First to say, "I told you so!" **Impact.** Participants feel dismissed and discouraged. Meeting is delayed and outcome may not be reached.	• Separate idea generation from discussion. • Stick to the agenda. • Seek their ideas.

Type	Behavior and Impact	Development (Tips to Improve the Situation)

Meeting Dominator	**Behavior.** Interrupts. Holds separate conversations. Bulldozes views.
	
	 Impact. Team members are afraid to ask questions and challenge ideas.
		• Enforce:
		  • 5-minute rule.
		  • One voice at a time.
		  • No interruptions.
		 • Have them write their ideas on paper and review with them individually.

The Disengaged	**Behavior.** Doesn't contribute ideas even when asked. Withdraws his/her effort and becomes silent. May use cell phone or laptop during meetings. Talks to neighbor while others are speaking. **Impact.** Team members may think that they want the project to fail. Facilitators may feel that they are not interested and stop calling for their contributions.	• Encourage and recognize contributions. • Define ground rules, and encourage group to endorse them. • Use techniques that require everyone to contribute. • Try breaking into small groups to encourage participation. • Meet 1-on-1 to find out if the person is aware of the behavior and its consequences. • Invite them to permanently withdraw from group if appropriate. (Maybe they really shouldn't be there!)

Type	Behavior and Impact	Development (Tips to Improve the Situation)
The Conflict Inducer	**Behavior.** Disagrees with most or all ideas presented by others. **Impact.** Participants feel unsafe, become discouraged, and stop contributing. Desired outcome is not reached.	• Ask for commitment on open-minded, ego-free approach. • Create collaborative environment. • Enforce ground rule that we disagree with ideas, not people. • Remind group of brainstorming rules to go for quantity, not quality. • Separate idea generation with idea selection. • Remind group that all ideas will be evaluated at a later time, and invite conflict inducer to wait until that time before dismissing others' ideas. • Use disagreement to develop better ideas. • Use time out to clarify concerns.

Type	Behavior and Impact	Development (Tips to Improve the Situation)
The Techie Talker	**Behavior.** Uses a lot of acronyms and doesn't offer explanations; may appear arrogant. **Impact.** Business people afraid to ask questions. They may be confused but afraid to appear ignorant. Participants then shut down.	• Define ground rules about use of acronyms and technical terms and get group to endorse them. • Encourage questions from others. • Focus on project and organizational goals and how technical solutions help solve business problems.

TABLE 26: Common Difficult Stakeholder Types

Remember that the behavior needs to be observable rather than a judgment or perception. We want to be sure not to pre-judge a stakeholder who has proven difficult in the past.

 # *Summary*

- In this chapter, we discussed why some stakeholders seem difficult, what they want, and what we can do to lower their frustration.
- Finally, we provided a list of difficult stakeholder types, their behavior and impact, and some tips for how we can improve the situation.

1. I once was in charge of eliminating an organization's mail department. Of course I could not promise that no one would lose their jobs. I explained the project goals and why it was important to the organization. I answered all questions as they arose. It was interesting to see that many of the employees in the department were fully engaged in the project. Others were resistant and did what they could to prevent the inevitable closing. Interestingly, the organization found jobs for those who supported the change and helped the project. And the department head, who was instrumental in the project's success, was promoted - Elizabeth.

2. Note: The model used in this class is different from the SAFE model for stabilizing crisis situations. That model as accessed on July 11, 2012 in http://safehostage.com/ pdfsafe_model.pdf is used to negotiate hostage situations in an article by Mitchell R. Hammer, Ph.D., An Incident in Bowling Green, Kentucky.

Epilogue:
Putting the Influencing Formula Together

To be truly effective, we need to combine courage with trust and with preparation. Courage without adequate preparation makes us look foolish. We have lots of examples of this in our careers. Here is one example. Elizabeth was invited to and attended a meeting with about 20 business Subject Matter Experts.

"The meeting was taking a direction I didn't think was helpful. I asked a question. The meeting stopped and 20 pairs of eyes turned around and glared at me. There was absolute silence for what seemed like an eternity. Finally someone spoke up and said, "Elizabeth, we've already thought of that." The meeting then continued as if I had not said a word. My first reaction was to be embarrassed. I would gladly have crawled under the table. Later I got angry. I asked myself how I could work in an organization where they wouldn't even let me ask a question. "They wouldn't let me…"– one of those barriers to courage.

"However, the more I thought about it, the more I realized that I wasn't prepared for the meeting. Even though I hadn't received an agenda, I certainly could have prepared for the meeting by taking the initiative to meet individually with some of the participants prior to the meeting. I could have asked what would be discussed in the meeting. Surely if I had asked several of the participants, they would have provided things such as the purpose, desired outcome and topics, as well as what they wanted from me."

Courage without trust, on the other hand, is just plain foolhardy. It's the rashness we mentioned earlier. It is like going into battle alone with no one to support us. We may have solicited support from others who may have even promised their support.

However, doing battle without trust means that we take the proverbial arrows, while those we thought supported us stand on the sidelines cheering us on (or more likely simply watching and waiting for the inevitable disaster).

We need all the elements in the Influencing Formula to be able to influence without authority, as summarized below. We hope this "formula" proves helpful to you, whatever your need for influencing happens to be. Please refer to Appendix B for additional resources as you continue on your journey towards being a trusted advisor.

Figure 30: The Influencing Formula

Appendix: A

101+ Questions to Elicit Requirements and Uncover Expectations

When eliciting requirements and uncovering expectations for a project, much of the challenge stems from learning what the business needs from the new product being built. (The product is the end result of the project, such as a system, new equipment, new or changed process, new service, etc.) Oftentimes, we may not even know the right questions to ask to get started, much less get into enough depth to discover all the important needs of stakeholders. This handy guide is a summary to help you get started with your questions and to help ensure you've asked the important ones on a project.

General Requirements and Expectations Questions

1. Ask for trios, such as:
   - Why/why not/why now
   - What/what not/what now
   - Who/who not/who now

2. Paired extremes, such as:
   - Best/worst
   - Longest/shortest
   - Easiest/hardest

TIP

This article is also available along with many others on our website at: www. watermarklearing. com/articles.php.

3. Volumetrics, such as:
   - How many
   - How often
   - When

4. Avoid:
   - Can/could/should
   - Leading questions, such as
   - "Have you ever thought about a…"
   - "Isn't it better to…"
   - "Don't you think that…"

*Note: The interviewer will obtain better results if the interviewee feels safe.

Philosophy Towards Requirements

1. How will you determine that the requirement has been achieved? What are the acceptance criteria? How would you test?
2. Ask about use of the product (system).
3. Why and how is the product used?
4. What does it do for you/other systems/other business lines with which it interfaces?
5. How do you use the product in relation to the business steps/processes that you perform?
6. Under what conditions might the product not perform as planned (exception processing)?
7. Currently, under what conditions does the product not perform according to your expectations: time of day/week/month/year? Functions that you perform? Data you try to access? Amount of data you are transferring?

8. Dependencies. Can you give instances when a function or part of a function must be completed before another starts?

9. What are the physical environments in which the system is going to be used by the customers, such as dark/dirty/dusty/hot/cold/hazardous (chemical or radioactive)?

10. What are the physical limitations of the product, if any (such as space/height/weight/cable runs/capacities)?

11. What are the deployment requirements, such as pilot/parallel/switchover/iterative releases?

12. What are the safety requirements of the product?

13. What are the 7 x 24 availability requirements? When will the customers not use the product?

14. In what ways, if any, does the system have to be accessed by special needs people (age/mental capabilities/different cultures)?

15. What regulatory or legal agencies or bodies have an interest or set of requirements/rules related to this system?

16. What are the system interfaces?

17. What would be considered less than reliable availability of the system or product?

   a. Percentage (ex., 99%)

   b. Transactions or query loads

   c. Planned maintenance

   d. Mean time between failures (MTBF) or mean time to repair (MTTR)

18. Who will use the product and when (ex. internal/external/PC-literate/routinely or occasionally)?

Closing Questions

1. Is there anything else I should know about...?
2. What else should I know to make this project a success?

Other Fundamental Questions

The Ws: why, what, who, when, where. These questions are the fundamentals of requirements analysis. They help the analyst determine root causes, what the requirements are, who the stakeholders are, when processes occur, and where information comes from and/or goes to.

Who

- Who can provide information?
- Who else can provide information?
- Who else might be affected by this project or product?
- Who has authority to make decisions?

What

- What is causing the problem(s)?
- What would your ideal solution(s) look like?
- What are the benefits of this project?
- What is the priority of this requirement?
- What concerns do you have about...?
- What are your most pressing issues?
- What concerns do you have about the change or new product?
- If the system is not installed properly, what will your major concerns and pressing issues be?

Why

- Why was this new product or change requested?
- Why is this new system or change required?
- Why is this level of service required (response time, when reports are due, etc.)?
- Why is the system the way it is (whatever you observe or are told about)?

When

- When do you need this by?
- When is this system brought up in the morning and down at night?
- When do processes occur?

Other

- How much can we spend?
- How many resources are available? Who/what are they?
- When will they be available?
- Can the information you are giving me be shared with others?
- Are your answers official (or off the record)?
- How often is the system available/unavailable?

Data View Questions

Entities or classes

1. What are the categories of data (entities/classes), such as Customer?
2. What are the different types?

Entity (Data) relationship rules

1. Can one entity exist or be set up without a related entity (optionality rule)? For example, can a customer be set up without an account?
2. What are the minimums and maximums for the above? (How many customers can own an account/how many accounts can each customer own?)
3. If I {create, read, update, or delete} one entity, will there be an effect on another entity (referential integrity rule)?

Attribute and attribute rules

1. What are the facts (attributes) about each entity?
2. What, if any, are the domains (ranges/permitted values) of each attribute?
3. Is there intelligence built into the attribute and what are the consequences or impacts of removing it?
4. Is the attribute required or optional?
5. What flags or defaults are required?

Security and retention

1. How long does this data need to be retained?
2. Do you want it inactivated before deleted?
3. Who can read it?
4. Who can access it?

For data entry:

1. How/how often do you enter this information?
2. Who enters this information?
3. Who currently provides it?
4. Who needs this information?
5. Who gets this information?

6. Why do you need these inputs?
7. What information do you need in that report or on that on-line screen or window?
8. What information are you going to send (and to whom)?
9. What response time is required?
10. What is the current response time?

For reports:

1. How/how often do you analyze information?
2. Why does {business area} need this information?
3. How/how often do you summarize it?
4. How often do you produce this report?
5. How/how often do you report on it?
6. How often do you really need this information?
7. If you could, how often would you send it?
8. How often would you view it?
9. How often would you act on it?
10. How often would those you send it to do anything with it?
11. What information are you going to produce and for whom?
12. What information are you going to receive and by whom?
13. Who analyzes this information?
14. Who makes decisions with this information?
15. Why is information reported this way?
16. When are these reports generated?
17. When do you need to produce this report?
18. What information is contained in that report/user interface?
19. What information do you send (and to whom)?
20. What information do you receive (and from whom)?
21. What information do you produce (and for whom)?

Process View Questions

1. How do you get from point A (input) to point B (output)...?
   - What are the current process steps (as-is)?
   - What will the new process steps be (to-be)?

2. Ways or media (such as online, by phone, in-person) to:
   - Process
   - Receive
   - Distribute

3. Who is (what role or function) involved in the processing of ...?

4. Trigger questions
   - How often (do/receive/distribute)
   - When (do/receive/distribute)

5. How is something:
   - Created
   - Read or accessed
   - Updated or changed
   - Deleted or archived or purged

Interaction View Questions

1. What triggers the interaction?
2. What do we expect the system to do in response?
3. What notification comes back?
4. What do we expect the system to do?
5. What is the most common way to get to the end result?
6. What are some different ways to get to the end result?
7. What prevents you from getting to the end result?

Appendix: B
Additional Resources

As a training company, Watermark Learning is dedicated to increasing the knowledge and skills of project professionals around the world. In addition to our books and training classes, we provide a number of resources on our website at no charge. Once you register as a member of our learning network, you will have access to:

- **Templates**: Many of the tools and templates referred to in this book. We have over 50 different downloadable templates for influencing, project management, business analysis, and business process management.
- **Articles:** We provide over 100 articles and short tips of interest to project professionals. Our categories include: Influencing, Agile, Business Analysis, Business Process Management, Eliciting Requirements, General and Industry Trends, Project Success, and Requirements Management.
- **Webinars on Demand:** Our popular webinars on current topics are available to view as recordings. There are over 14 webinars and we add them as we give them, generally once per month. Earn PDUs and CDUs for re-certification as you watch them!
- **Miscellaneous:** We provide a number of certification resources for PMP, CBAP, and CCBA certification. There are links to professional and industry resources, and extensive bibliographies of recommended books.

Visit **www.watermarklearning.com/resources** today and register to start taking advantage of these great resources!

Instructions for Downloading Templates Referred to in this Book

- Visit www.WatermarkLearning.com.
- If not already a member of our learning network, register as a member using the **Become a member** link in the upper right-hand corner of the home page.
- Click the **Resources | Templates** menu item and log in.
- Scroll through our list of templates, categorized by:
    - **Business Analysis** – templates focused on requirements-related work and other templates of interest to business analysts, including CBAP® and CCBA® certification.
    - **Business Process Management** – templates to help you model, analyze, design, and transform business processes.
    - **Influencing** – many stakeholder templates are listed in this section.
    - **PMP Certification templates** – as the name implies, these worksheets will help you prepare for your PMP® exam.
    - **Project Management** – templates focused on project management work.
- Click the "**Download**" link for the template you want to download, and it will be delivered to your desktop.
- See the next page for a list of templates referred to in this book that you can download and use instantly. The list includes templates that weren't mentioned in this book, but might prove useful for your influential preparation.

TEMPLATE	FORMAT*	PURPOSE
Communication Style Analysis	PDF	A visual summary of a personality framework/ communication style that revolves around two basic dimensions: Task-oriented vs. people-oriented. Internally-energized vs. externally energized.
Decision Tree	PPT	A tool that can help frame alternate recommendations and show possible outcomes.
Fishbone Diagram	PPT and Viso	Visual "cause and effect" diagrams to explore causes of a problem or opportunity at a high level, using a small number of cause categories.
Pareto Diagram	Excel	Graphically show the most significant contributors to a problem, ordered by their frequency from highest to lowest. Illustrates the "Pareto Principle," or the 80-20 rule. Includes a data area for input and a chart to use with the data.
Process Map	Viso	A sample swimlane diagram to use for any process mapping, including the process diagram root-cause analysis described in this book.

TEMPLATE	FORMAT*	PURPOSE
Process Scope	PPT	When formulating recommendations, this chart provides a visual summary of what is in scope.
RACI Responsibility Assignment Matrix	Word	Role and responsibility matrix, indicating who is Responsible for something, who is Accountable, who to Consult with, and who to Inform.
SARIE Consulting Summary	PDF	A quick summary overview of the SARIE consulting process.
SARIE Form	Word	A simple template to record each point of the SARIE consulting process.
Selection Matrix/ Payoff Matrix	Word	A matrix to guide implementation efforts by structuring recommendations according to how beneficial they are and how easy they are to implement. Template records the decisions.
Stakeholder Analysis (Influence-Acceptance Matrix)	PPT	Shows organizational influence in relation to the likely acceptance of the final outcome. Use this grid if you feel there is resistance to the product or project or if there is potential sabotage.

TEMPLATE	FORMAT*	PURPOSE
Stakeholder Influence Analysis Matrix	Doc	A way to analyze stakeholders by categorizing them by their influence in the organization compared to what we need during projects.
Stakeholder Registers	Two types:	Contains output from categorizing stakeholders and consolidates information about key stakeholders, including both categorization and contact information.
1) Stakeholder Classification Worksheet	Word	Groups stakeholders by key categories to help manage large groups and ensure compete requirements.
2) Stakeholder Contact Worksheet	Word	Lists stakeholders with contact information. Useful to keep in contact with stakeholders and to track the groups they belong to and their role.
Weighted Ranking Matrix	Excel	A technique that combines pair-matching with weighted criteria to help objectify a decision or recommendation.

*Software required to use templates: Excel = Microsoft Excel (.xls), PDF = Adobe PDF, PPT = Microsoft PowerPoint (.ppt), Word = Microsoft Word (.doc)

Index

About the Authors

Elizabeth Larson, PMP, CBAP, CEO, and Richard Larson, PMP, CBAP, President of Watermark Learning (www.watermarklearning.com).

With over 30 years of project management, business analysis, and consulting experience each, they have presented workshops, seminars, and training classes on five continents. They have built and managed all aspects of Watermark Learning for over 20 years, including the development of training curriculum, instruction, sales, marketing, and operations. Their articles have appeared in CIO Magazine and they have been featured in PMI Network.

The Larsons were both lead authors of the *PMBOK® Guide* 4th edition (Collect Requirements) and Elizabeth is the content lead for Scope Management for the *PMBOK® Guide* 5th edition. Both Elizabeth and Richard were lead contributors to the (*BABOK® Guide* v. 2.0). Elizabeth and Richard co-authored the *Practitioner's Guide to Requirements Management* and the *CBAP Certification Study Guide 2.0*.

The Larsons are proud grandparents of five lively grandsons. They love to travel and have visited over 35 countries around the world. Both are certified as Project Management Professionals (PMP) and as Certified Business Analysis Professionals (CBAP). Their company was awarded the PMI® Education Product of the Year for 2011.